Try Your Hand at This

Easy Ways to Incorporate Sign Language into Your Programs

Kathy MacMill

THE SCARECROW PRESS, INC.
Lanham, Maryland • Toronto • Oxford
2006

SCARECROW PRESS, INC.

Published in the United States of America
by Scarecrow Press, Inc.
A wholly owned subsidary of
The Rowman & Littlefield Publishing Group, Inc.
4501 Forbes Boulevard, Suite 200, Lanham, Maryland 20706
www.scarecrowpress.com

PO Box 317
Oxford
OX2 9RU, UK

British Library Cataloguing in Publication Information Available

Library of Congress Cataloging-in-Publication Data

MacMillan, Kathy, 1975-
    Try your hand at this : easy ways to incorporate sign language into your programs /
Kathy MacMillan.
        p.   cm.
    Includes bibliographical references and index.
    ISBN 0-8108-5447-3 (pbk. : alk. paper)
    1. Libraries and the deaf.   2. Libraries and the hearing impaired.   3. American
Sign Language—Study and teaching.   4. Children's libraries—Activity
programs.   I. Title.
    Z711.92.D4M33   2006
    027.6'63—dc22   2005018799

To Mom and Dad,
because of . . . well, everything.

Contents

~

Foreword

Try Your Hand at This: Easy Ways to Incorporate Sign Language into Your Programs by Kathy MacMillan is a very helpful and user-friendly guide for librarians and other library personnel involved in library programming. She's "been there and done that," and it shows. From how to set up programming involving sign language for all ages—from babies to adults—to dealing with and paying interpreters, publicizing programming both to the public and within the deaf community, and evaluating and improving the library's sign language collection, Kathy MacMillan knows what she's talking about. Her understanding and knowledge of the deaf community and the importance of sign language to this community are particularly impressive, and she explains these concepts well. She's also good at handling the numerous erroneous myths about deafness and sign language that are, unfortunately, still often perpetuated.

This book is a worthy successor to *Library Services to the Deaf and Hearing Impaired* by Phyllis I. Dalton, published in 1985. The Dalton book was an excellent resource at the time, and I was very pleased to have it available to me during my years as librarian for the deaf in the District of Columbia Public Library System, but it is now dated. Also, Kathy MacMillan has had considerably more direct experience with deaf people and sign language than Phyllis Dalton did when she wrote her book (e.g., MacMillan is studying for a degree in American Sign Language interpreting, while Dalton did not know sign language). This is not to minimize the importance of the earlier book, which can be said to have led the "first wave" in this area, but now it is time for a "second wave," and *Try Your Hand at This: Easy Ways to Incorporate Sign Language into Your Programs* is an excellent start.

Despite her long experience and extensive studies, Kathy MacMillan has been able to keep her book clear and accessible to those without experience in this field, an impressive accomplishment. It is all too easy for those who have come a long way to lose touch with the needs of those starting out. This she has managed to avoid. Those with more experience will find her suggestions useful "checklists" because she is also good at handling details, such as things to remember when using interpreters and the differences between interpreters and skilled signers.

Kathy MacMillan is clearly aware of the importance of marketing library programming directly to deaf people themselves. This book gives library staff helpful approaches for drawing deaf people into the library. For example, where possible, it is very helpful to have people with sign language skills available. Sign language programs, such as those the D.C. Public Library started for its staff, are useful. Another suggestion, which I can second from personal experience, is to hold sign language programs at the public library for people—both deaf and hearing—who want to learn sign language and about Deaf Culture.

On a personal note, Friends of Libraries for Deaf Action, which I founded in 1986 with the support of volunteers at the D.C. Public Library, is now going online. While this is a work in progress, our information service, *THE RED NOTEBOOK: Deaf Awareness Begins @ your library*, will be adding the names of library friends and organizations that are willing to work with their local public libraries to promote accessibility and quality library resources for all—deaf and hearing. Check www.folda.net to find out the latest!

Congratulations to Kathy MacMillan for her useful and interesting book. I predict it will have a long and welcome presence on library staff book-shelves.

Alice L. Hagemeyer, MLS
Founder of Friends of Libraries for Deaf Action (FOLDA)

Acknowledgments

First and foremost, I would like to thank Corinne Vinopol and the Institute for Disabilities Research and Training, Inc., for their extraordinary support and encouragement of this project, as well as for providing the graphics for the ASL glossary. Thanks also to Alice L. Hagemeyer for her support and feedback; Chris Wixtrom, whose enthusiasm and love of sharing resources led me to many of the wonderful items mentioned here; Debby Parker and Lynne Erb, who gave valuable feedback on early drafts; Jan Kehrli, Amber Haslinger, and Claudine Hanner, who provided last-minute reference assistance; the staff of the Carroll County Public Library, Eldersburg Branch, who processed holds on countless books for me while I was creating the bibliography for this book; T. J. Waters, who has been my sounding board and confidante through so many projects; and the students of the Maryland School for the Deaf, Columbia Campus, who inspired many of the programs in this book. I'd also like to thank Liz Sabine and Ian Galloway, without whom this book would never have become a reality. Last but not least, I thank my husband, Jimmy, who suffers my long hours of muttering and poring over the keyboard with patience and understanding.

~

Introduction

Perhaps you've seen it on the bus, on the street corner, in a restaurant. Or maybe you went to a play and couldn't stop watching the interpreter. You might have checked out a book or video from your library to learn a few signs, or perhaps you even registered for a class. Whether you learned about it once in the Girl Scouts or interact with deaf people on a regular basis, odds are you've seen and been interested in sign language at some point and even thought, "Wow, I wish I knew more about that." After all, American Sign Language (ASL) is, according to common assertions, the third or fourth most-used language in the United States. Unfortunately, because it is not recognized as a foreign language on censuses and other surveys, this statement is difficult to prove with hard facts.

American Sign Language is more than just an assortment of gestures. It is a full-fledged, unique language, with all the characteristics of such. It has probably never occurred to you to introduce sign language into your programs the way you might incorporate Spanish or French or German. Maybe the idea is even a little intimidating. Not to fear—this book will guide you through the common pitfalls of new learners, give you the background knowledge necessary to introduce ASL in context, and offer practical suggestions for adding value to *any* program by including signs. You'll find everything you need to get started right here, including guidelines for establishing partnerships in your community, working with interpreters, and marketing your programs; a visual glossary of commonly used storytime signs; and a bibliography of resource books. And once you're ready to put it all into practice, you'll find a trove of sample programs for all ages, as well as annotated bibliographies of picture books, music, and games to use with sign language to help you develop your own programs.

I started incorporating simple signs into my programs while taking my very first ASL class back in the autumn of 1999. At the time, I was a children's librarian in a public library, and I was amazed at how well even hearing babies responded to the use of basic sign language. Since then, I have presented hundreds of programs for young children, elementary school kids, and teenagers about sign language, but I also continue to incorporate signs into programs I present on other topics. Though my primary work now is with deaf children, I continue to present programs to hearing audiences in public libraries, and sign language is always a part of them, no matter what the topic or the target age group. Though I began doing this while working toward a degree in ASL interpreting, you don't have to go to school to use sign language in your programming; all you need is a positive attitude, an open mind, and this book!

Usage Note

Throughout this book, I have represented American Sign Language signs and phrases through the use of glossing, or presenting the most closely equivalent English word in capital letters. In cases where more than one English word is required to describe the ASL sign, those words are joined by hyphens (e.g., I-LOVE-YOU).

PART I

MAKE YOUR PROGRAMS SPARKLE WITH SIGN LANGUAGE

Learn how using sign language can make your programs more popular, participative, and fun, as well as a host of techniques for incorporating signs into programs and connecting with a wider audience.

CHAPTER ONE

Sign Here Please

Who is so deaf or so blind as he that willfully will neither hear nor see?

—Sixteenth-century English proverb

Using sign language in your programs does far more than just spice them up. You can use sign language to offer your program attendees cognitive benefits, to increase your program attendance, to support multicultural goals, to welcome deaf patrons, and even to give your programs an edge on the competition.

Signing Is Good for the Brain

Imagine this: An eight-month-old girl is hungry. But she doesn't cry to get what she wants, thereby sending her parents into a tizzy of wondering whether it's a "feed me" cry or a "change my diaper" cry or a "pay attention to me" cry; she merely looks at her mother and signs MILK. Mother knows what to do, and both adult and child have avoided frustration through communication.

It's a scene that really happens throughout the country; maybe you've even witnessed it in your storytimes. With the soaring popularity of Joseph Garcia's *Sign with Your Baby* and such baby-sign videos as the *Signing Time* series, more and more hearing parents of hearing children are using sign language with their infants to increase communication and avoid frustration.

Research shows that early use of sign language has other benefits as well. Babies have the conceptual ability to comprehend and use language long before they develop the skills to speak, so real communication in sign can occur as much as a year before speech. Also, recent brain research supports the idea that exposure to *any* foreign language in the first few years of life increases the ability of the brain to learn new languages later on because the supporting networks of neurons and synapses have already been established in infancy. Using American Sign Language with babies not only makes it easier for them to learn the language later but also makes it easier for them to learn *any other* language, including English, because it stimulates the language centers of the brain. The need for early exposure to ASL becomes even more vital for deaf babies, who do not receive the auditory exposure to English in their early years that hearing babies do and whose overall language skills will suffer if they do not see lots of signing early on. Results of studies at the University of California show that babies who learn sign language score higher on IQ tests and have larger vocabularies in both spoken and sign languages later in life.[1]

The benefits of signing are not limited to babies. Jan C. Hafer and Robert M. Wilson of Gallaudet University have conducted extensive research on the use of sign language to support reading instruction. Because it helps children form mental pictures of printed words, utilizes multiple senses, and provides additional motivations for learning, sign language can supply a strong support system for education. Hafer and Wilson identify several groups who can benefit from the use of sign language as reinforcement in reading instruction, including beginning readers, remedial reading students, learning disabled students, and students of English as a second language.[2]

And It's Fun Too

Fortunately, using ASL in your programs is so much fun that kids won't suspect for a minute that it's also good for them! Kids of all ages are invariably fascinated with sign language. (Adults too—offer a sign language program and you will be surprised at how many adults will stay who might otherwise have taken the time to search for books without the kids in tow.) If you don't believe that, go take a look at the sign language materials in your collection—that is, if you can, since most of them are likely to be checked out.

Public librarians often field questions from kids and parents about where to find sign language classes for children. Unless you live in a highly unusual community, you won't find many opportunities out there. Occasionally you will see a sign language camp offered by a recreation and parks department, and some high schools are starting to offer ASL as a foreign language, but very rarely are ongoing classes geared to elementary school children. In fact, most sign language classes are available in community colleges and universities, and kids with a thirst for the language have few opportunities to develop their interest. The kids who *do* learn sign language are usually those lucky enough to have a deaf relative, friend, or neighbor who teaches it to them.

No matter, you think—they can just learn it from books and videotapes, right? Not so fast. First of all, ASL is a visual, three-dimensional language, which makes learning signs from the static images in a book difficult at best. The larger problem, though, is that misconceptions about ASL and deafness abound in our culture, and an appalling number of well-meaning but ill-informed books and videos have made their way onto library shelves. These productions share one major flaw: they present ASL completely apart from its context and history and fail to treat it with the respect one should accord to any foreign language. We'll discuss the common misconceptions about ASL and deafness at length in chapter 3, and you'll find tips for bringing your collection up to date in chapter 7.

The point is that you will have a ready-made audience for using sign language in your programs because kids are already fascinated by signs and have few outlets for that interest. However, because of the common misunderstandings about sign language in our culture, you will need to be very careful about presenting the language in context and treating it with the respect it deserves. It's not nearly as difficult as it sounds—you're already on your way!

ASL Supports Multicultural Learning

If you're like most hearing Americans, you've never heard of Deaf Culture, the idea of ASL as a completely separate language from English surprises you, and you're thinking how odd it sounds that I just referred to you as a "hearing person." Most likely, you've never really thought about any of these things before. American Sign Language is a unique language, with its own grammar, structure, and syntax *and* its own cultural base of users. Because of the visual-gestural nature of the language, most people don't realize this; linguists, in fact, did not begin to study ASL seriously until the 1960s.

Maybe you picked up this book thinking that using signs in your programs could promote deaf awareness, in terms of disabilities. But incorporating sign language into your programs promotes multicultural awareness as well. If you present ASL *in context*—that is, with an understanding of the Deaf Culture behind it—you will increase children's knowledge of the world around them and most likely give adult attendees a few surprises as well!

At least 140 colleges and universities accept ASL for fulfillment of foreign language requirements, and many high schools are following suit.[3] Think about it: American kids are far more likely to come into contact with users of ASL in their lives than they are to meet French or German speakers (depending on your location, of course!). By introducing even a few ASL signs in your programs, you are offering children valuable communication tools they most likely will not receive elsewhere.

Everybody Wants to Sign

Sign language is far more versatile than other languages because you can use it in any program, with any age group. It instantly makes any program more interactive and engages participants. Even babies can understand and begin to produce signs. (And even those too young to produce signs will benefit from exposure to them.) Toddlers and preschoolers benefit from the use of signs to focus their attention and emphasize language concepts. Even the most rambunctious school-age kid will sit still to sign, learning something about relating to other people in the process. And middle schoolers, that hardest to reach of age groups, respond to focusing prompts in sign language that would cause them to roll their eyes if delivered in English. Even those talkative parents who sit in the back of your storytime room will pay attention when you demonstrate signs, especially because they will often have to help young children perform them.

Using sign language also supports the goals of programming for each age group. For babies, sign language incorporated into stories, fingerplays, and rhymes encourages parent–child interaction and stimulates language development. Sign language in toddler storytimes focuses attention on important concepts and encourages active participation in language. In preschool storytimes, which are usually a child's first independent experience, sign language can be used most effectively to establish routines and expectations, encourage responses to books and stories, and broaden children's knowledge base. For elementary school children, sign language can be used in all of these previous ways, but also as a means of exploring the languages, cultures, and feelings of others. For middle schoolers, this concept can be extended even further, allowing children to explore the language and its cultural background in more detail and to overcome prejudices. In every case, using sign language in your programming furthers the library's mission of disseminating knowledge and promoting greater understanding in our communities.

Welcoming Deaf Patrons

Deaf people traditionally have not been great users of libraries, due in part to their lack of awareness about what the library can provide for them, but also due to a lack of awareness on the part of librarians about their needs.

Perhaps you often provide interpreters for library programs—that's great, but if the topics and formats of those programs don't fit with what your deaf patrons want, then it won't matter.

Incorporating sign language into your programs probably won't cause deaf patrons to flock to your library, but it *will* open a door. By signing in programs, you will create an awareness of sign language and deafness. You will acknowledge the value of sign language and will encourage other staff and patrons to become interested in it as well. Deaf parents who have hearing children will feel more welcome to bring their children to storytime. Deaf kids in the program will also benefit if you use their native language, even a little. (Even if you have an interpreter there, use sign language with the whole group. The deaf patrons will love it.) Think of it this way: Suppose you're visiting another country and do not speak the language, and you go to a program where someone makes an effort to teach the other attendees a few words of your native tongue. Wouldn't you be pleased? Many deaf people see that kind of attempt made so rarely that, when it happens, especially in an institutional setting such as the library, it comes as a pleasant surprise.

Even if you never learn more than five signs—even if you read this book only once, use a few of the baby programs, and then relegate the book to the "maybe I'll do more with it later" pile—you will have started to make a difference. By approaching ASL and deaf people in an open and respectful manner and sharing that approach with the children in your programs, you have modeled an important attitude that we see far too rarely. In fact, an astounding number of librarians fail to meet the needs of their deaf patrons simply because they *do not think to ask what those needs are.* I can tell you the primary need right now: an honest willingness to take the time to communicate, whether it be through signing, through an interpreter, through telephone relay, or through writing notes back and forth. If you've taken the time to learn how to properly add signing to your program, you have already taken the first step toward closing the gap between deaf and hearing people.

A "Hand Up" on the Competition

Let's face it, libraries are no longer the only game in town. We've all seen increased competition from chain bookstores, recreation and parks programs, and even fast-food restaurants that have started offering storytimes and family events as a way to get people in the door. Library programs, we like to think, are the real thing, and none of these mercenary endeavors could possibly offer what trained librarians, familiar with the broad range of literature, could. That may or may not be true, but the sad fact is, people don't always realize what they've got in their libraries. (For instance, how many of your patrons even know that a master's degree in library science exists, let alone whether or not you have one?) Competition for people's leisure time is fierce, and it's no longer enough for libraries to depend on memories of beloved childhood books and kindly old librarians to get people in the door.

Programming for all ages has become increasingly important as a means of attracting families and enticing difficult-to-reach age groups into the library. Consistent use of sign language in your programs adds value to your story-times, and word is sure to get out, even if you don't advertise. If you *do* advertise, even better! What a great tidbit to mention to a reporter: "Oh, we always teach at least two signs in our Toddler Time program. . . ." Add a fact sheet about the benefits of signing with babies, gleaned from some of the resources in the bibliography of this book, and you just might wind up on the front page! Such a hook might be just the thing to draw in groups such as homeschoolers, who often seek out programs with educational benefits.

The primary value that sign language will give to your programs, though, is that they will instantly become more interactive as you teach the signs and encourage children to use them again and again. This may sound self-evident, but an astonishing number of programs simply go from book to song to rhyme without involving the participants at all, as though the storyteller is the performer and the children are the passive audience. Of course, if you have been doing programming for a while, you probably already know a host of techniques for drawing kids out and encouraging them to participate in stories. It's time to add sign language to your storytime arsenal!

Notes

1. Joseph Garcia, *Sign with Your Baby* (Seattle: Northlight Communications, 1999), 24.

2. Jan C. Hafer and Robert M. Wilson, *Signing for Reading Success* (Washington, D.C.: Kendall Green Publications, 1986), 2–3.

3. Sherman Wilcox, "Universities that Accept ASL in Fulfillment of Foreign Language Requirements," at www.unm.edu/~wilcox/ASLFL/univlist/univlist.html (accessed October 18, 2003).

CHAPTER TWO

"But I Don't Know Sign Language!"

It's not always a hearing person's ASL skills that are essential to being accepted by DEAF people. Attitude and effort are much more important.

—Gil Eastman, deaf actor and author

Anyone Can Learn ASL

If you can learn French or Spanish or German, or even learn a few vocabulary words in those languages to enrich your storytimes, then you can learn ASL. On the other hand, becoming fluent in ASL takes years of study and practice, just as with any language. Some people think that knowing the manual alphabet and a few signs means they're fluent, mostly because of misconceptions about ASL's status as a language, which will be discussed more in depth in chapter 3.

Whether your goal is to become fluent in American Sign Language or just to learn enough to serve your patrons better and add interest to your programs, opportunities to learn the language abound. Luckily for you, ASL is more accessible than ever, thanks to a growing number of classes and learning materials.

The Many Avenues to Learning ASL

Books

For librarians, books are often the most obvious route. But beware—since ASL is a visual, three-dimensional language, two-dimensional illustrations and descriptions do not do it justice. Just trying to follow the motion lines in many ASL dictionaries can give you a headache. Books can do a great job of describing the structure and background of ASL (see appendix A for some suggestions), but actual vocabulary is best learned in other ways, at least initially. Many students find dictionaries and other ASL vocabulary books a great reference tool to remind them of signs they have already seen.

Remember that ASL follows a totally different structure and grammar from English, so you can no more learn it out of a dictionary than you could formulate sentences in German by making a word-for-word correlation out of a German/English dictionary. Vocabulary is just vocabulary, without grammar and structure—which may be all you need if your goal is to incorporate a few signs into your storytime.

Another caveat: beware of outdated books. Many books written in the 1980s and earlier espouse outmoded ideas about the deaf community and present hearing people's views of the language rather than the actual language itself. (See chapter 7 for tips on updating your collection.)

Classes

Classes are the most intensive way to learn the language and naturally require a certain time commitment. If you really want to develop conversational skills, however, classes are the way to go. Most community colleges offer at least ASL I and II; if you find a school near you that offers an interpreter training program or deaf studies program, you may be able to take classes up to ASL V or VI. Local recreation and parks departments often offer ASL classes as well, though the quality of these may be harder to judge.

The major benefit of classes is that many are taught by deaf teachers— native users of the language. Whether the teacher is deaf or hearing, however, most serious classes will be taught completely voices-off, meaning that students are expected to communicate through gesture and writing until they pick up the signs. This approach keeps the focus on the concepts and the signs, rather than on the English word equivalents that many hearing people obsess over, and leads to a more natural internalization of the language.

Videos and DVDs

The past few years have seen an explosion of sign language videos on the market—some quite good, some simply cashing in on a popular phenomenon. Video meshes well with the visual nature of ASL and is far more successful at conveying the nuances of three-dimensional language than books are. Another advantage of video is that users can learn at their own pace, rewinding and watching again if they miss something.

If you are lucky enough to have access to a library that owns the ASL Access collection—a collection of more than two hundred ASL videos, including instructional, children's, poetry, and more—then make use of those resources. To find out about obtaining the collection for your library, visit www.aslaccess.org. Even if your library can't afford the price of the entire collection, the reviews on the website are an excellent guide to the best American Sign Language videos.

If your goal is to learn signs for baby or toddler storytimes, then you can't do better than the *Signing Time* video and DVD series. Geared to preschoolers, this series contains basic vocabulary from a child's world, demonstrated by adults and children, and even includes signed songs and activities that could be incorporated into storytimes.

Computer Software
Recent years have seen a variety of ASL dictionaries and other interactive software products on the market. While these programs may share the drawbacks of books—many use line drawings that can be difficult to read—they often incorporate technologies such as streaming video to demonstrate the signs more accurately or offer special printing features that can be useful for developing program materials. The major producer of ASL software products is the Institute for Disabilities Research and Training, Inc. (www.idrt.com), which provided the graphics for the ASL glossary in appendix E of this book.

Deaf Friends, Family, and Patrons
If you're lucky enough to have a deaf friend, deaf family member, or deaf patron willing to teach you ASL, then don't turn down the opportunity! Having that personal connection to the language may keep you more motivated than formal classes or self-guided learning from books or videotapes, and you will be learning from a real live person. Like any living language, ASL changes and adapts with the people who use it, so the signs you learn from an actual human being are much more likely to be accurate and up to date than those found in books. Of course, this way of learning may also prove more informal and haphazard, depending on your motivation and that of the person teaching you. If you meet with your sign language coach once a month to learn a list of vocabulary but don't practice in between, don't expect to retain the information! Like any language, you will lose it if you don't use it.

So how do you determine the best method of learning more signs? It depends on your goals. If you want to become fluent in the language, taking a class or finding a tutor is the best way to go. If your goal is only to learn a few signs to use in programs, then videos and books, supplemented by support from a fluent signer, may be enough. And there's nothing wrong with the latter goal—just recognize it and be honest with yourself about what you can and can't do.

Why Context Is Key

Whichever method of learning you choose, it's vital that you understand the background of the language you have chosen to share. You would never dream of injecting a few French words into a story while completely ignoring the fact that there's a country called France. But too often, sign language is presented without any mention of deaf people, Deaf Culture, or even the understanding that it *is* a language. As librarians and teachers, we have a responsibility to share the correct information, especially because so much ignorance about deafness exists in our society.

It can be a challenge, yes. As Harlan Lane notes in his foreword to *For Hearing People Only* (a highly readable, incredibly informative introduction to deafness and Deaf Culture), Deaf Culture tends to be invisible, and hearing people tend to think that they already know everything they need to know about deafness: "Whereas few Americans construct for themselves an image of Hispanic culture (for example) by extrapolating—by imagining themselves with mastery of the high-school Spanish and a meal ticket to Taco Bell—most Americans do construct their idea of the lives of Deaf people by extrapolating—by imagining themselves without hearing."[1]

All this is not meant to put undue pressure on you or to discourage you from using sign language in your programs. Just make sure that you represent the language in a balanced, accurate way, and you'll enrich not only your young patrons' language but their worldviews as well.

A Note about Regional Variations

Many new learners are confused by the regional variations in American Sign Language—which, when you think about it, are as natural as a Philadelphian ordering a "hoagie" while a New Englander orders a "grinder." Though mass media has contributed to greater standardization of American English, such a change is slower in coming to a language with no written form. (This may change in the future, however, with the increased use of video communications technology among deaf Americans.) Differences between the East and West Coast signs tend to be most dramatic (e.g., in California, the sign for *computer* is a C handshape signed at the forehead; on the East Coast, it is a C handshape moving several times up the opposite arm).

Don't be surprised if you run across such variations when using signs—and for goodness' sake, don't tell a deaf person that his or her sign is wrong because it doesn't appear in your book! Remember that ASL is a living language and is used differently in the real world from how it is written down in books, just as spoken English is not a direct transcript of a grammar textbook.

How Acknowledging Deaf Culture Sets You Apart

Most hearing people have never even heard of Deaf Culture, and the very concept that deaf people could be anything other than disabled is foreign to them. For most people, this attitude exists not because they are mean or ignorant but simply because they've never been exposed to the idea before. It doesn't help that most materials focusing on sign language in the past have downplayed Deaf Culture or ignored it entirely. By demonstrating even a basic awareness of Deaf Culture in your use of signs in your programs, you will provide a context for parents and kids alike, teach the hearing people in your audience something new, and show respect for the language and its native users.

Attitude Is Everything

Some hearing people worry that deaf people will resent them for trying to learn their language, especially if they want to use it for a narrow purpose (such as programming). It's true that some deaf people resent hearing people "co-opting" their language, likely because many hearing people approach learning ASL as a charity enterprise—they want to "help the poor deaf people." When you consider how often the average deaf person has likely encountered such a patronizing attitude in his or her life, it's no wonder that one might be suspicious of new learners and their motivations.

If, however, you approach the language—whatever level of involvement with it you decide to pursue—as an adventure in learning, as an opportunity for you to learn something new and share the exciting things you learn with others, as a way to open up communication with a bunch of neat people you have never been able to communicate with before, and with a willingness to listen as well as talk, you'll quickly defuse any negative reactions you might encounter.

Note

1. Matthew S. Moore and Linda Levitan, *For Hearing People Only* (New York: Deaf Life Press, 1993), 7–8.

CHAPTER THREE

What You Never Learned in School

You would think the accident would have narrowed my world, limited me. It did the opposite. I started to pay attention to the world instead of taking it for granted.

—I. King Jordan, first deaf president of Gallaudet University

What Is Deafness?

Dictionary definitions of deafness tend to focus on its audiological aspect. Consider the following:

"The lack or loss of the ability to hear."[1]

"Partially or wholly lacking or deprived of the sense of hearing; unable to hear."[2]

"Partially or completely lacking in the sense of hearing."[3]

As the Harlan Lane quote in the last chapter sums up so well, hearing people tend to focus on what deafness *isn't* rather than what it is—what deaf people seemingly lack instead of what they have, what they can't do instead of all the things they can. Deafness is therefore defined as an inability to hear or a *lack* of hearing. But this only gives a part of the real picture.

People commonly begin their questioning about deafness by asking what causes it. I offer here a list of some of the possible causes of deafness, only because it is a common question, not because it will tell you anything real about deaf people. Some of the common causes of deafness include genetic factors, accidents, constant high noise levels, illness, infections, and rubella or other viral infections contracted during pregnancy.[4]

Medical definitions of deafness, however, will get us only so far. Relying solely on such information is like saying that Pygmies are nothing more than people who lack height and ignoring their entire culture, history, and language. The *American Heritage Dictionary of the English Language* offers an alternative definition, not based on hearing or lack of it, and one that gets closer to the truth:

"Of or relating to the Deaf or their culture."[5]

Deaf with a Capital D

You might have seen the capital-d "Deaf" before and wondered what the capital letter meant. Most hearing people, when asked to guess, will say that it has something to do with degree of hearing loss—which is, when you consider it, an entirely hearing way to think. To most deaf (and Deaf) individuals, degree of hearing is less important than it is to hearing people, and far less important than language, culture, and place in the community.

Lowercase-d "deaf," then, refers to the general condition of being deaf, as defined by the dictionaries and medical community—the lack of hearing. Uppercase-d "Deaf" encompasses far more; it stands for Deaf Culture and beliefs, as well as the idea that deaf people can do nearly anything that hearing people can do. Culturally Deaf people do not consider themselves broken or impaired in any way and often resent being called disabled.

American Sign Language is a central value of Deaf Culture. Acceptance into Deaf Culture has far less to do with hearing or lack of it than it does with mastery of ASL, a belief in the abilities and talents of deaf people, and sharing the core values of the culture. Deaf Culture is a fascinating, multifaceted topic to explore; to learn more about it, seek out some of the resources listed in appendix A.

The most important thing to remember is that deafness is about seeing, not lack of hearing. As George Veditz, president of the National Association of the Deaf, said in 1913, "They are facing not a theory but a condition, for they are first, last, and all the time the people of the eye."[6]

A Brief History of American Sign Language

The story of American Sign Language is, for better or worse, closely tied to the history of deaf education in the United States. In the early 1800s, there was only one place in America where a large group of deaf people, and therefore a sign language, existed: the island of Martha's Vineyard, off the coast of Massachusetts. Long before it became the popular vacation spot it is today, Martha's Vineyard was a small enclosed society of whalers and sheep farmers, and nearly everyone on the island, whether hearing or deaf, knew and used the local sign language. One of the original island settlers was deaf, and the trait was passed down for two hundred years in the small island community, where people rarely moved off-island. Deaf people were completely integrated into the community. Most notable is the fact that the islanders did not seem to realize that the presence of so many deaf people was in any way unusual, even though one out of every five children was born deaf in the village of Chilmark.[7]

Elsewhere in the United States, deaf people had a much more difficult time of it. The lifestyle of the times meant that most deaf children, born to hearing parents, lived in isolated rural areas or small communities and often went their whole lives without seeing another deaf person. Most communicated with their families using gestures and made-up home signs. Those lucky enough to have wealthy parents might be sent to Europe to a school for the deaf; no such schools were yet available in the United States.

That changed, however, when Thomas Hopkins Gallaudet met a young deaf girl named Alice. Fascinated by her obvious intelligence, he discussed her education with her wealthy father, Dr. Mason Fitch Cogswell. The two men realized that the problem of education for deaf children needed to be addressed, and they gathered a group of concerned citizens to study the issue. In the summer of 1815, the group sent Gallaudet to London to gather more information from the Braidwood School, a well-known school for deaf children that many wealthy American deaf children attended. The Braidwood School was known for using only the oral method—speechreading and speech, but no sign language.

Once in England, however, Gallaudet found that the Braidwoods refused to share their methods with him unless he promised to stay for several years at the school and swore not to reveal any of their techniques to others. He attended other lectures on education—mostly pertaining to hearing students—and was ready to leave in discouragement when he attended a lecture given by three men from the Royal Institution for the Deaf in Paris. Abbé Roche Ambrose Sicard, the hearing man who ran the school, demonstrated his school's success by inviting audience members to ask questions of the other two men, Jean Massieu and Laurent Clerc, both former students who had become teachers at the school. Sicard would interpret the questions into French Sign Language, and then the two men would respond by writing in French on a chalkboard. The audience members were shocked that the deaf men could even read and write, let alone answer deep philosophical questions on topics such as religion, philosophy, and education.

Gallaudet knew he had finally found what he'd been looking for. He approached the three men, and they invited him to come to Paris and study at their school, where they would happily share their methods. He studied at the school for several months but rapidly became homesick. He did not want to give up his mission, but he knew he had to return to the United States soon.

In May 1816, Laurent Clerc offered him a way out—and changed the course of American deaf history—when he volunteered to accompany Gallaudet back to the United States to help found the school. Clerc was not only an excellent teacher but also an inspiring success story; raised in a small village in the south of France, he had not known any form of real communication before the age of twelve, when he arrived at the Paris school. He achieved a teaching post just eight years later.

Clerc and Gallaudet sailed to America in 1816, using the time on the journey to teach each other their languages; Clerc taught Gallaudet French Sign Language, and Gallaudet tutored Clerc in reading and writing English. The first permanent school for the deaf in the United States (and, indeed, in the entire western hemisphere), the Connecticut Asylum for the Education and Instruction of Deaf and Dumb Persons, opened in Hartford, Connecticut, on April 15, 1817. Like most schools for the deaf in this country, both then and now, it was a residential institution. Later renamed the American School for the Deaf, it is still in operation today.

Students came from all over the country to attend the school, and what we know as American Sign Language was born from the confluence of the French Sign Language taught by Clerc, the Martha's Vineyard Sign Language brought by the many students from that island, and the various home signs brought by other students. In the rich soil of a community of users, the language flourished. The approach at the Connecticut institution was decidedly manual; unlike the leaders of London's Braidwood School, Gallaudet and his peers saw no need for speech or speechreading and championed instead the "natural language of signs."

Many other schools for the deaf opened their doors in subsequent years, often filling their teaching posts with graduates from the Connecticut institution. The years between 1817 and 1880 were a sort of golden age for the deaf community in America.

Then, in 1880, everything changed. A worldwide conference on deaf education was held in Milan, Italy, that year. It would later become known, infamously, as the Milan Congress. The majority of attendees came from France and Italy, where oralism had come to dominate deaf education. The American delegates numbered only five (one of them, James Denison, was the only deaf delegate in the entire convention), and they stood nearly alone in their belief that sign language was the best way to educate deaf children. Decrees issued by the congress stated the "incontestable superiority of speech over signs" and that "the method of articulation should have the preference over that of signs in the instruction and education of the deaf and dumb."[8]

It was not the first time that the use of sign language in American schools for the deaf had been challenged—Alexander Graham Bell, a heroic inventor to so many Americans, had long been an enemy to deaf signers because of his vocal and pervasive beliefs about the superiority of speech and his advocacy of laws preventing deaf people from marrying each other. The Milan Congress, however, put the international stamp of approval on oralism. In the way that such educational theories often do, this notion spread like wildfire, and soon deaf teachers were being fired to make way for hearing educators, many of whom could not even communicate with their students. One can only imagine how the students must have felt, trying vainly to learn through speechreading a language they had never heard.

American Sign Language did not disappear, however. It survived, for eighty long years, in the secret of dormitory conversations, and flashed back and forth behind the backs of oralist educators. Many of the dismissed deaf teachers became dormitory counselors, and so deaf children still had deaf role models who signed. ASL remained the active language of the deaf community; oralism could batter it but not break it.

Not until the 1960s did linguists come to the aid of ASL. William Stokoe published his *Sign Language Structure* in 1960, proving that American Sign Language, and indeed, all sign languages, have a linguistic basis just as spoken languages do.

Following Stokoe's research, the education pendulum began to swing back toward sign language—but not all at once. Some educators began to use total communication (TC) in the 1960s and 1970s, which combined signs and speech. The idea was to address the various needs (and hearing levels) of children in the classroom by signing in English word order while speaking at the same time. This led to the development of various forms of Signed English, which uses ASL signs in English word order (often adding suffixes and other invented signs to represent those word parts that have no equivalent in ASL). The success of Signed English is debatable, but what is certain is that it is *not* a language but a means of representing English on the hands.

In more recent years, beginning in the late 1980s and early 1990s, many schools have adopted a more balanced approach, known as bilingual biculturalism. In this method, ASL is used as the primary language of instruction, and written English is taught alongside it. ASL and English are presented as equal but separate languages, with respect for both. Hearing culture and Deaf Culture are recognized as separate but coexisting entities. Many schools today provide speechreading and speech training by parental request, but these are separate services from the main instructional track.

The history of American Sign Language, though it goes back only about two hundred years, is full of twists and turns of joy and sorrow and is essentially the story of the oppression of deaf people in this country. Given this history, it's easy to see why many deaf people are fiercely protective of their language.

Why ASL Is a Real Language

William Stokoe's research in the 1960s changed the way people understood ASL and signed languages in general. Previously, sign languages were seen as somehow lesser, more primitive and animalistic; unfortunately, such misconceptions persist even today. Stokoe promoted a new way to look at sign languages and proved that they have distinct grammar and syntax. Instead of morphemes, phonemes, and the other units of sound that make up spoken languages, sign languages consist of five parameters, or parts: handshape, movement, location, palm orientation, and nonmanual signals. The last parameter, often underestimated by novices to visual language, is arguably the most important. Nonmanual signals include facial expression, body shift, and other parts of a sign not found on the hands. This separate grammar and structure means that it is impossible to sign ASL while speaking English because the two are completely separate.

What Do Interpreters Do?

The job of a sign language interpreter is to facilitate communication between deaf and hearing people. That means the interpreter is there as much for the hearing person as for the deaf person; if everyone in the situation used ASL, then the interpreter wouldn't be necessary. So the often-used term "interpreter for the deaf" is incorrect. It's important to note the distinction between "signer" and "interpreter"; a signer is someone who knows how to sign, while an interpreter knows how to interpret between two languages. Becoming an interpreter takes years of training and practice beyond simply becoming fluent in ASL. For more information about hiring interpreters and working with them in your programs, see chapter 7.

Ten Common Misconceptions about ASL and Deafness

Myth 1: All deaf people lipread. Perhaps Hollywood is to blame for the persistence of this idea among hearing people—movies and television rarely show a deaf person who *doesn't* "read lips." In fact, the correct term is *speechreading* because the process involves watching the mouth, neck, and facial expressions, as well as considerable use of context clues. Speechreading is a difficult skill to master, and most of the time it's actually easier for hearing people to learn. Don't assume that any deaf person can speechread—but don't assume they don't either. Many profoundly deaf people can speechread common phrases such as "May I help you?" When in doubt about the best way to communicate with someone, ask.

If a deaf person is trying to speechread you, the worst thing you can do is exaggerate your speech or talk very slowly. Simply enunciate clearly and speak at a normal speed and volume, and make sure to maintain eye contact.

Myth 2: All signs are like pictures in the air. Many ASL signs do seem to look like what they represent. The sign ELEPHANT, for example, shows an elephant's trunk. But assuming that all signs in a visual language *look* like what they mean is akin to assuming that all words in a spoken language *sound* like what they mean. Many signs have nothing to do with their meanings at all, just the same way that most English words are arbitrary collections of sounds that have come to mean certain concepts. Sometimes signs begin in an iconic fashion and then soften into something more arbitrary through use; a good example is the sign for HOME, which originally combined the signs EAT and BED. Through time and use, the sign slurred into what it is today, and the origins are still recognizable if one knows to look for them, just as is the case with many English words.

Myth 3: Deaf people read braille. Now, you're probably thinking, "That's an obvious myth!" But you'd be surprised how many hearing people unthinkingly lump deafness and blindness together. As a librarian at a school for the deaf, I constantly heard, "Oh, so all your books must be in braille." It's quite possible that the two are linked so closely in the minds of many hearing people because of Helen Keller, the famous deaf-blind woman, and often the only major deaf figure that hearing people can name. To set the record straight, deaf and blind are very different things. Blind people generally use English and are part of hearing culture. And braille is a form of communication that makes the written word accessible to blind people—it is *not* a language as ASL is.

As for deaf-blindness, that's a whole separate issue. Many deaf-blind people use tactile signing as Helen Keller famously did. A large percentage of deaf-blind people have Usher's syndrome, which means they were born deaf and then lost their sight later in life. This means that ASL is usually their first language, so tactile signing is a natural progression for them. However, there are many causes of deaf-blindness, and the only certain thing is that you can't make generalizations about deaf-blind people and their preferred communication methods.

Myth 4: *It is possible to sign American Sign Language and speak English at the same time.* As we have seen already, English and ASL are separate languages with distinct grammatical structures. It would be just as impossible to sign intelligible ASL and speak intelligible English simultaneously as it would be to write intelligible Spanish and speak intelligible English simultaneously—your brain simply can't do it, at least not without a lot of practice.

But wait, you say—I've seen people signing and talking at the same time before. What you've seen is not ASL but Signed English—a system that uses some ASL signs but in English word order. Signed English is not a language of its own; it is a system for representing English on the hands. Many deaf people can understand Signed English but much prefer the more visually attuned ASL.

Myth 5: *"Hearing impaired" is a nicer term than "deaf."* We use a lot of euphemisms in our society: "disabled," "physically challenged," and the like. To many hearing people, saying "deaf" just seems so . . . direct. "Hearing impaired" is certainly the more politically correct term, right?

When you think about the values of Deaf Culture, however, it's easy to see why many deaf people take offense at the term "hearing impaired." It implies brokenness and impairment where culturally Deaf people see only a language and cultural difference. "Deaf" is a perfectly acceptable term—and unlike "hearing impaired," it's not a term that has been imposed on the deaf community from outside. Though certainly some deaf people may consider themselves hearing impaired, "deaf" is generally the safest term to use.

Myth 6: *All deaf people want cochlear implants so they will be able to hear.* The most recent technological breakthrough affecting deaf people is the cochlear implant. This electronic device is surgically implanted in the inner ear and activated by a device worn outside the ear. Unlike a hearing aid, which merely amplifies sound, the cochlear implant converts sound into electronic signals that are sent directly to the auditory nerve, thus bypassing the ear. With training and support, the cochlear implant can allow some deaf people to have partial hearing.

To many hearing people, it seems a given that deaf people would want to be able to hear. Unfortunately, the promises made by the medical community have not always happened in reality—cochlear implants are not the miracle solution they first appeared to be. The implantation process involves several stages and requires years of therapy and support, and often children with cochlear implants never develop intelligible speech.

On top of all that, many deaf people don't really care much about hearing in the first place—if you don't see yourself as broken, why would you need to be fixed? Some deaf people even see cochlear implants as an insidious plan by the hearing medical establishment to destroy Deaf Culture. The truth is most likely somewhere in the middle. Misunderstandings about Deaf Culture and deaf people persist, particularly in the audiologically focused medical community.

Myth 7: All deaf people use their hands to communicate. Just as deaf people vary greatly, so do their communication methods. It's fairly safe to say that those who consider themselves culturally Deaf use American Sign Language. But many deaf people use some form of Signed English, or a blend of ASL and Signed English. Many others speechread to varying degrees and use speech to talk to others. Many deaf people use a combination of these methods, giving precedence to whatever works in a given situation. Communication is the primary goal, and most deaf people develop a repertoire of ways to achieve it.

Myth 8: Sign language is universal. This misconception stems from a basic misunderstanding of the fact that sign languages are languages. Many hearing people think that sign language is a universal set of gestures. This couldn't be further from the truth. Many different sign languages exist all over the world, including British Sign Language, Chinese Sign Language, and Zimbabwe Sign Language. All of these sign languages are independent of the spoken languages in their native countries. Though American English and British English are closely related, American Sign Language and British Sign Language share no such relation. ASL is actually most closely related to French Sign Language because of the history discussed earlier in this chapter. American Sign Language is used throughout the United States and Canada.

Many people ask if there is a universal sign language. The answer is "sort of." Gestuno, or International Sign Language, is a limited set of established signs, supplemented by gestures, that is used at international conferences of deaf people. It is similar to Esperanto in that it is used only in a very limited setting—international meetings—and does not fit the definition of a true language.

Myth 9: Deaf people are more likely to have deaf children than hearing people are. It seems a natural assumption that deaf parents are likely to have deaf children, but in fact, 90 percent of deaf children are born to *hearing* parents.

This fact accounts for the language delays that many children face. Because they are not exposed to any language from birth, many deaf children arrive at school with poor language skills, and they struggle with learning. English is notoriously difficult for deaf people to learn because many do not have a strong foundation in their first language (ASL) before trying to learn English as their second. Sadly, a shocking number of hearing families either don't sign at all or don't sign well enough to fully communicate with their deaf family members.

Deaf children of deaf parents have an immediate advantage—they are exposed to a rich, complex language from birth and absorb it just as naturally as hearing children absorb spoken language. Studies have shown that deaf children of deaf parents tend to succeed in school, have better social skills, and possess higher-level language skills than their counterparts with hearing parents.[9]

Myth 10: Teaching sign language to young children will cause speech delays. One of the great myths spread by the supporters of oralism in the late 1800s was that use of sign language would impair speech ability. Unfortunately, this misconception has persisted today; some parents worry that using sign language with their hearing or deaf baby will somehow block a child's ability to learn speech. Studies have shown that this assumption is patently untrue. In fact, early use of sign language with both hearing and deaf children has been shown to increase their speech abilities later because it stimulates the language centers of the brain and develops neural pathways.

So Much to Learn

Is your brain full yet? This has been just a taste of the many surprising facts about sign language and deafness. If you'd like to explore any of these topics further, check out the resources listed in appendix A.

Notes

1. *American Heritage Stedman's Medical Dictionary* (Boston: Houghton Mifflin, 2002), 210.

2. *Random House Webster's Unabridged Dictionary* (New York: Random House, 1997), 512.

3. *American Heritage Dictionary of the English Language* (Boston: Houghton Mifflin, 1992), 466–67.

4. "What Causes Deafness?" Laurent Clerc National Deaf Education Center, at http://clerccenter.gallaudet.edu/about/faq.html#deaf4 (accessed December 29, 2004).

5. *American Heritage Dictionary of the English Language*, 466–67.

6. Jack R. Gannon, "History through Deaf Eyes," at http://depts.gallaudet.edu/deafeyes/ (accessed December 29, 2004).

7. Nora Groce, *Everyone Here Spoke Sign Language: Hereditary Deafness on Martha's Vineyard* (Cambridge, Mass.: Harvard University Press, 1985), 53–94.

8. John Vickrey Van Cleve and Barry A. Crouch, *A Place of Their Own: Creating the Deaf Community in America* (Washington, D.C.: Gallaudet University Press, 1989), 110.

9. Harlan Lane, Robert Hoffmeister, and Ben Bahan. *A Journey into the Deaf-World* (San Diego: DawnSignPress, 1996), 27.

~

CHAPTER FOUR

Seven Simple Techniques for Incorporating Sign Language into Any Program

Those who will not learn to communicate with others are truly handicapped.

—Gil Eastman, deaf actor and author

Now that you know some background information about American Sign Language and the people who use it, it's time to start using those signs to spice up your programming! This chapter focuses on easy ways to use sign language in any program, with any topic. Chapter 5 discusses developing and presenting programs about sign language and deafness.

Technique 1: Use simple signs to emphasize your theme. All good programmers use various presentation styles, such as flannelboards, books, songs, and fingerplays, to lend variety to their programs. Learning signs can be a fun activity in its own right. Pick two or three signs that relate to your topic and teach them to the group. Make sure to allow ample time for little fingers to make the signs, and check to make sure everyone is signing the signs correctly. Sometimes it helps to describe the signs as you make them. For example: "This is the sign for dog. Do you see how I pat my leg and snap my fingers as if I am calling a dog?" Try to explain the signs in words that will be meaningful to your audience.

When introducing signs in your program, be sure to emphasize that you are using American Sign Language and not just making up gestures. Some children may never have heard of American Sign Language; others will be eager to show you all the other signs they know. Here are some ideas for how to introduce the concept of American Sign Language:

> "I am going to show you another language now. (Show sign.) Does anyone know what language I'm using?"
>
> "This is American Sign Language. Do you know who uses American Sign Language? . . . Right, people who can't hear. But people who *can* hear can learn sign language too."

A minimal explanation such as this is all that is needed for programs for young children or programs where your focus is on something other than sign language. But it's important to give a context for the language, for all the reasons discussed in earlier chapters.

To emphasize your theme, choose signs relating to your topic. You can teach signs at the beginning of your program (often the best place if you plan to use them in other activities), in the middle as an interactive stretch, or as a finale. Because performing the signs requires the attention of both hands and eyes, introducing the signs can be a great way to recapture the wandering attention of a group in the middle of storytime. Next time a group gets too loud to raise your voice over, try turning your voice off entirely and just signing a few signs. The kids will be so curious to know what you're doing that they will settle down quickly.

How do you choose which signs to introduce in your program? For younger children, it's often best to start with signs for concrete objects or activities, especially if you plan to use the signs in other activities throughout the program. Look through appendix E for ideas. For older children and family programs, you could also include letters of the alphabet and more advanced concepts, such as "love" and "friendship." Here are some examples to give you an idea:

> A program about elephants: ELEPHANT, GRAY, PEANUT, E
> A program about friends: FRIEND, PLAY, I-LOVE-YOU
> A program about bedtime: GOOD-NIGHT, KISS, SLEEP, MOON
> A program about fall: TREE, LEAF, SQUIRREL, FALL
> A baby program: HELLO, BABY, MOTHER, FATHER

Technique 2: Use simple signs in fingerplays and rhymes. Most programs for young children will include at least one fingerplay or rhyme, and coming up with hand motions to accompany the rhymes and make them interactive can sometimes be a challenge. Using signs in the place of made-up hand gestures makes the rhymes interactive *and* introduces a new language all at once. Fingerplays are an ideal place to introduce signs because they rely on repetition, giving children multiple opportunities to practice their new signs. You can use signs that you introduced earlier in the program, or introduce the signs specifically for the fingerplay. It's best to teach the signs separately before starting the fingerplay, and then tell children to sign when they hear the appropriate words. Also feel free to incorporate gestures into fingerplays as well.

Here's an example:

> The elephant is big and gray.
> He stomps his way through town.
> The elephant swings his trunk way up,
> And then he swings it down

In this example, you could sign ELEPHANT each time the animal appears in the rhyme, and then stomp to show how the elephant walks. Then you could use your arm to show the trunk going up and down. For older children, you also might want to introduce the signs for BIG and GRAY.

One caveat about using signs in fingerplays: For rhymes with long-established hand motions, such as "The Itsy Bitsy Spider," trying to introduce sign language will probably just cause confusion, especially among very young children. For those kinds of rhymes, it's probably best to stick to tradition!

Technique 3: Use signs for counting and colors. Counting and color signs are some of the most versatile storytime signs and can be incorporated easily into almost any program. Flannelboard rhymes and fingerplays often include counting in their structure. By using the American Sign Language numbers, you'll reinforce language as well as counting skills. Also, because counting is used so often in storytimes, regular attendees will be exposed to the language repeatedly. You will definitely want to explain that you are using ASL numbers when you do this because most people will not even realize it—or may even complain that you are holding up the wrong fingers for the number three! In addition, counting in ASL is a simple and subtle way to include any deaf participants who may be in your group.

Colors also appear often in flannelboards and other rhymes. Teaching the signs for various colors, then asking the children to repeat them, is an easy and effective way to make even the most boring flannelboard more interactive.

Technique 4: Use ASL as part of a standard opening or closing routine. Whether you see the same group at storytime every week or you offer drop-in storytimes with rotating participants, you probably have your favorite ways of opening and closing a program. The younger the child, the more important structure and repetition become, and establishing standard routines can make everyone feel more comfortable, including the presenter.

Consider incorporating ASL phrases such as HELLO, GOODBYE, and I-LOVE-YOU into your opening and closing routines. A silent, very large HELLO signed in a roomful of talking storytimers can be a very effective means of gaining a group's attention. See technique 6 for ideas about incorporating signs into opening and closing songs.

Technique 5: Use signs for group management. We've all experienced a rambunctious group of kids who won't settle down, no matter how many times we utter the plaintive "Let's all pay attention now" in our best happy-librarian voices. We've tried all the tricks—addressing kids by name, shifting group focus—but sometimes the group energy is still off-kilter.

Sign language can be a very effective way of redirecting the group's attention and bringing everyone back together. Used over time, the signs become effective reminders of target behaviors. Also, for children with behavior issues such as attention-deficit/hyperactivity disorder (ADHD), signs offer a visual reinforcement of verbal prompts and address different styles of learning. At the very least, seeing the signs may distract children from the disruptive behavior.

Surprisingly, sign language prompts work just as well with older children as they do with younger children. In fact, they may even begin policing each other by using those signs. I used signs such as PLEASE, TOGETHER, and PAY-ATTENTION with a group of middle and high school volunteers at a public library and found that they responded consistently to the signed prompts without any of the eye rolling that would have resulted from verbal prompts. They found the sign language so neat that they forgot to be too cool to behave.

Which group management signs you use and how you introduce them will depend on the age group of your program. For an older group, or a group you will be working with for some time, it's a good idea to establish the ground rules up front, using the signs as you do so. Then, when they see those signs later, they will recognize them. For younger children, you may want to introduce the signs as you need them so they will be surprising enough to distract from unwanted behavior. See the Group Management Signs section in appendix E for illustrations of appropriate signs to use.

Technique 6: Use signs in familiar songs. Songs form a part of almost every storytime. Often, we struggle to make them interactive. Sign language is, of course, an easy and effective way to do that. You could incorporate signs such as HELLO and GOODBYE into standard opening and closing songs that you already use. This would reinforce the signs each time you use them, and repeat storytime visitors will delight in showing off what they've learned.

You can incorporate signs into other songs as well. Familiar songs are generally best because that way you and your participants don't have to worry about remembering the words *and* the newly learned signs. Don't worry about signing every word in the song. While it is possible to sign songs, any attempt to do a word-for-word interpretation of a song into ASL will end up mangled; as we saw in chapter 3, ASL and English have different structures. At this point, it's best to teach one or two signs and incorporate them into the song. As with fingerplays, you can supplement the signs with gestures.

Here's an example:

> "Sticky Bubblegum" (traditional)
> Sticky sticky sticky bubblegum,
> Bubblegum, bubblegum.
> Sticky sticky sticky bubblegum
> Sticking my nose to my knee.
> (Repeat ad nauseum, sticking other body parts together.)

This song could be done with the signs for STICKY and CHEWING-GUM repeated with the words, along with using gestures to show the sticking of body parts. (Incidentally, this is a great song to use in family programs and with older kids—all ages seem to enjoy it equally!) For more ideas for incorporating signs into music, see the annotated discography in appendix B.

Technique 7: Use signs in stories. Whether you're reading a story from a book, telling it with props or a flannelboard, or outright telling the tale, signs are a quick way to involve your audience in the story. Stories that use repetition are best—choose a couple of words or phrases from the story, teach your audience the signs at the beginning, and then have them sign each time they appear in the story. Be careful not to overwhelm your audience; don't try to use more than three or four new signs in one story, or the effect may be diluted.

Sign language is also a great way to present wordless picture books in storytime. A book such as Eric Carle's *1, 2, 3 to the Zoo* is a great way to introduce animal signs, and the pictures reinforce the concepts. Plus, it gives you something to do with the book if you're not sure what to say. See appendix B for an annotated list of recommended books to use with sign language.

Putting It All Together

These are the seven basic ways to incorporate sign language into any program, but they don't have to be separate. You could introduce three or four signs at the beginning of your program, then use them throughout in stories, songs, and fingerplays, supplemented by counting and group management signs. The sooner you start, the easier it is to continue, and the sooner you will see kids' (and parents') enthusiasm for sign language. Using sign language on an ongoing basis in your programs, even in the minimal ways described here, will add a dimension to your programs that participants will remember long after the last page has been turned and the last silly shaken out.

CHAPTER FIVE

Hands-On Sign Language

Do you ever wonder why people say that a person's eyes, not the person's ears, are the window to the soul?

—Gil Eastman, deaf actor and author

As we've seen, it's easy to incorporate a little bit of American Sign Language into any program, with any topic. But suppose your patrons want more? In fact, once you start using a few signs to spice up your regular storytimes, you're likely to hear comments such as, "I wish you offered programs that teach more sign language!"

Interest in learning ASL has grown exponentially in recent years, among all age groups. The increased visibility of signers on television shows such as *Blue's Clues* and *The West Wing* only feeds this trend. Parents are just as interested in learning sign language, in most cases, as their kids are. In fact, many parents see learning sign language as a family affair—something the whole family can do together.

Your library is in a prime position to offer high-interest programs because very few opportunities exist for kids to learn sign language. Programs that offer even basic sign language instruction for whole families are almost impossible to find.

Identifying Your Audience

When developing programs about ASL, the first thing you need to do is figure out who your target audience is. You may already know this information, based on listening to your patrons' comments or feedback on surveys. (It may even be what spurred you to pick up this book!)

If you aren't sure which age group to target, first try incorporating some basic signs into your regular programs using the suggestions in chapter 4. Then observe which age groups respond with the most enthusiasm. This will tell you where your efforts at sign language programs will best be focused.

You might also opt to start out by offering family programs about sign language. This way, all ages are welcome, and you can monitor attendance to get a feel for which age groups might merit more targeted programs later. Of course, as anyone who has presented all-ages family programs can attest, this requires extreme flexibility and energy; you might need to change your program around at the last minute when you wind up with a preponderance of older or younger kids.

Regardless of which age group you decide to target, you are likely to get interest—and perhaps even attendance—from all ages. American Sign Language is a topic of such wide-ranging interest that older children and adults may not particularly care that your program is aimed at preschoolers—they're just interested in learning the signs. Likewise, parents with very young children may want to sit in on a program geared to elementary-age children or to teens in the hopes that their kids will pick up some signs. Remember also all those misconceptions about ASL; parents whose sole experience with sign language is storytelling videotapes may be unable to fathom that you might plan to discuss topics such as the history of ASL or Deaf Culture in a program for teens—topics unlikely to hold the interest of a squirming preschooler.

If you are planning to target your presentation to a specific age group, you may want to consider ways of limiting attendance, such as advance registration or tickets. At the very least, you will want to make very clear in your publicity which age group the program is intended for. Use your judgment, and be prepared to shift gears if you're faced with a roomful of people older or younger than what you expected.

Another factor to consider when developing your sign language programs is how you will format them. Will the program be presented as a one-time special? A two- or three-part series? A series running several weeks? This will determine how you select materials, how you advertise, and how people perceive your program. The longer a series runs, the more people will be expecting a "class" as opposed to a program. If you do not have the knowledge and comfort level to provide detailed ASL instruction, then you are probably better off limiting your programs to one-shot specials or two- or three-session series, allowing you to keep the focus on specific topics about which you've made yourself a temporary expert. The programs in this book will provide examples.

Selecting Program Materials
for Various Age Groups

Now that you've figured out your audience, it's time to gather your materials and put them all together into a coherent program. Some general guidelines for all sign language programs include the following:

- Keep it interactive! Alternate factual information with activities and signs.
- Don't pretend to know more than you do. If you're not sure about a sign, or the answer to someone's question, be honest.
- At the same time, don't be afraid to share what you do know from your reading. You don't have to be an expert to present this information. If you feel uncomfortable setting yourself up as an "authority," then refer people to the books listed in appendix A. Approach the programs with an attitude of "Isn't this neat? We're exploring sign language together."
- Let your enthusiasm for the language shine through. The more excited you are, the more excited your audience will be.
- Be flexible. If you feel that you're losing your audience, switch to a different activity, or try some of the group management signs discussed in chapter 4.
- Think about sight lines! Make sure everyone in the room can see you. If necessary, ask participants to sit in a circle, or ask people to move so that others can see. If people can't see your signs, they can't learn them.

Programs for Babies and Parents

Programs for this age group are most likely to focus on the baby-sign phenomenon. Interest among parents will likely be high, and many of them may already be using baby signs with their children. Because of this, you'll want to allow time at some point in your program for parents to discuss their own use of baby signs. An informal playtime for the babies after storytime is an ideal outlet for this.

You may want to keep the focus of your program broad ("Baby Signs") or narrow it down ("Bedtime Signs," "Baby Signs at the Zoo," and so on). Which approach you take will determine how you structure your program. Try combining basic baby storytime staples, such as familiar songs, props, flannelboards, and bounces, with a few simple signs worked into each activity. Choose signs for concepts that are a part of a baby's world. Use objects, such as balls, stuffed animals, and toys, to reinforce the meaning of the signs. Repeatedly show the objects, then the signs, throughout the activities.

Don't be concerned if the babies do not repeat the signs right away, and tell the parents not to worry about this either. Just being exposed to the signs will benefit the babies, and most will not begin to sign back for some time. If they do sign back, make sure to give lots of smiles and praise.

Offer information for parents while you are entertaining the babies. Give them ideas for how they can use the signs and activities during their daily routines (e.g., "This would be a wonderful rhyme to sign at bedtime"). Sprinkle factual information about the benefits of using sign language with babies throughout your program so that parents are not overwhelmed. See appendix A for resources to help you find this information.

You'll also want to briefly mention Deaf Culture to the parents; too many videos and books have jumped on the baby-sign bandwagon in recent years without once acknowledging the rich and complex nature of the language. Some of the books don't even use ASL at all but signs "based on ASL." Make sure to warn parents about this because most are probably unaware of the difference. A handout with the tips you've covered, as well as books and websites for further consultation, is a great way to end the program.

Programs for Toddlers and Parents

When planning sign language programs for toddlers and parents, you'll certainly want to follow all the general guidelines for successful toddler programs—keep the length manageable for short attention spans, keep the program moving, and keep it interactive. Teaching signs is a perfect way to make your program interactive throughout. Just make sure you pick signs that match up with a toddler's experience. For this age group, you'll want to stick to signs that represent concrete objects or easy-to-represent actions. Also, when choosing which signs to share with toddlers, keep in mind that little hands may not be able to form some signs or may not be able to form them exactly. Encourage parents to help their children make the signs, and tell parents not to worry if the children don't sign them exactly right. Just keep modeling the correct way, and the kids will eventually pick it up. Use each sign several times throughout your program for reinforcement.

As with baby programs, you may want to incorporate information for parents into your storytime. Offer ideas for using the signs and activities at home and throughout the day. Be sure to emphasize that American Sign Language is a language, and by teaching it to toddlers, parents will help their little ones develop linguistic abilities.

Programs for Preschoolers

Sign language programs for babies and toddlers often closely resemble regular storytimes, with the addition of signs used throughout and information geared to parents. For preschoolers, however, you can really start incorporating information about American Sign Language and deafness into your programs.

Be sure to start with a basic explanation so that everyone knows what you're doing. An explanation for this age group could be as simple as the following: "Some people are deaf. That means they can't hear. They use sign language to communicate. But anyone can learn sign language."

Choose stories that illuminate the deaf experience. (See appendix A for suggestions.) Share these with the children, and be sure to allow time for discussion afterward. This approach focuses not only on the language but also on the people who use the language.

Of course, you can also incorporate stories and songs that have nothing to do with deafness into your program, teaching signs to go along with them. Try to alternate new material with familiar songs and stories.

When deciding how to structure your program, think about how specific you want to get. "Let's Learn Sign Language" is a very general topic that would work well. If you want to narrow it down a bit, think about other topics that would appeal to preschoolers and how you could use those topics to teach sign language. For example, "Color Signs," "1–2–3, Sign and Count With Me," and "Summer Signs" would all be excellent narrow-topic programs. Whichever topic you choose, don't miss the opportunity to incorporate information about deafness and Deaf Culture in your programs. Keep the focus on empathy and understanding differences, and keep explanations simple.

Programs for Elementary School Children

Sign language programs for this age group are especially fun because the children are likely to have some prior understanding of deafness and some experience of sign language, however limited. Of course, this means that they are also likely to hold misconceptions about deafness and sign language. Be sure to begin with a general definition of terms such as *deafness* and *American Sign Language*. Structure this information in question and answer format so the kids have a chance to show off what they know.

Another reason programs for this age group can be so rewarding is that you simply have more time. The kids have longer attention spans and are able to pick up more of the signs without being prompted. You can also introduce interactive games that reinforce sign vocabulary and often require sustained voices-off periods. See appendix C for suggestions. (If you don't think the kids will turn their voices off for the games, try offering an incentive—give each participant tickets, and take away one ticket every time a person talks. At the end of the voices-off period, hold a drawing for small prizes using the tickets left. It works like a charm.)

It becomes easier with children at this age to incorporate information about the deaf experience. Many excellent picture books on the market today are perfect for this age group. Don't forget to leave time for discussion—the kids will have opinions and questions.

Consider using other storytime staples and incorporating signs into them as well—a craft using the I-LOVE-YOU sign is sure to be a hit, for example, or you could teach a familiar song such as "Happy Birthday" in ASL. Be sure to go slowly, repeat often, and leave plenty of time to practice.

Don't forget about homeschoolers. The educational quality of sign language programs is sure to appeal to homeschoolers, so let them know when such a program is coming up.

Programs for Teens

Teens are one of the most challenging audiences to program for, but they're also one of the most natural audiences for sign language programs. Middle and high school students often develop a keen interest in sign language, whether because of books they have read, television shows they have seen, or deaf people they have met. Members of Scout troops often learn a bit about sign language while completing a badge for communications or some similar area. Whatever the reason that draws them to it, teens who develop an interest in American Sign Language are often quite serious about their desire to learn more.

Sign language programming for this age group can be especially rewarding because you can go into more detailed explanations and present vocabulary in more depth than with other age groups. Also, teens tend to pick up the signs very quickly, so you can include more vocabulary in a session than you might include for younger, or even older, age groups. Teens are especially fascinated with cultural and historical information about deafness and sign language, which they may never hear elsewhere.

As with every age group, you'll want to make your program as hands-on as possible, with lots of opportunities to interact and practice vocabulary. In some ways this is easier with teenagers: they pick up the material quickly, can grasp rules to even complicated games, and are usually eager to use the signs and move around rather than sit and listen to a lecture. In some ways it is more difficult: teens may be reluctant to turn their voices off, or they may feel shy or silly about participating in some of the activities. For this reason, it's essential to do some sort of icebreaker activity before expecting teens to participate in sign language games. An icebreaker may or may not involve sign language and can be as simple as going around the room and asking everyone to introduce themselves and say why they are interested in learning sign language. Do some seated activities with the kids before launching into an interactive game—this will give more bashful participants a chance to feel comfortable with the group. For suggestions for icebreaker and other games to use in sign language programs, see appendix C.

As with younger children, it's important to give teens a chance to show you what they know. Many of the participants may know some signs already and want to share them. Build in opportunities for discussion and feedback.

A series of programs on various topics relating to sign language is ideal for teens. The best way to make sure you address what they really want to know is to ask them. At the first session, ask each person to write down one or more topics that he or she would really like to learn about. You may want to give them suggestions, such as animal signs, family signs, and so on. Then use this information to plan later sessions.

Another fun way to structure a series is to give the group an ongoing project in addition to the other activities you plan. This might be learning to sign a simple song or other standard items, such as the Pledge of Allegiance. You can find a good ASL interpretation of these things on a videotape and teach the group a bit each week. You might even stage some kind of performance of the project at the end of the series. An ongoing project such as this will keep kids coming back and will give them a definite sense of accomplishment at the end of the program.

Programs for Families

Programs geared to all ages may be among the most challenging to pull off but can be extremely successful if planned well. You can draw elements from the previous sections in your planning, but the most important thing to remember is to be flexible—plan several options for yourself. Be prepared to switch gears if your audience turns out to be overwhelmingly older or younger than you had anticipated. Keep the pace moving, and choose signs that can be performed by younger children.

In many ways, sign language is an ideal topic for family programs. As we have seen, people of all ages are fascinated with signing, and parents are more inclined to participate when they are learning something too. Older kids who might normally scoff at stories and silly songs will pay attention and get involved when there are signs to be learned; often, they will also hurry to assist the younger children in learning the signs.

Your explanations of language and culture will necessarily be truncated in a program such as this, where everything has to keep moving, but don't cut them out entirely. Parents and older kids will be interested in the information, and it's important to keep the language in context. You can adjust to the needs of your broad audience by sprinkling facts about Deaf Culture and history throughout your program.

Above all, when presenting family sign language programs, keep your sense of humor. Don't be afraid to use your group management signs, even on the adults!

Programs for Adults

As a librarian with a limited knowledge of American Sign Language, you're unlikely to be presenting to adults only. Some topics may lend themselves to these kinds of programs, though, especially topics involving using signs in parenting. Don't be afraid to teach basic vocabulary to a roomful of adults; most of your attendees will know few or no signs and will be fascinated to learn more. And don't be afraid to address misconceptions about deafness and American Sign Language; most hearing people hold quite a few that they are unaware of and will be glad for the opportunity to discuss the actualities of these issues.

Whether you are presenting to adults exclusively or not, they will undoubtedly be a part of your audience, no matter what age group you decide to target. (Even parents of teens are likely to ask if it's okay if they can sit in on the program.) Librarians often complain about the problem of parents sitting in the back of the room during storytime and talking, disrupting the program. This is rarely a problem with sign language programs because the parents are just as eager to learn as the kids.

The biggest problem with adults in sign language programs is that they may feel silly and reluctant to really participate. I usually address this problem at the beginning of a program if I feel it will be an issue. I teach the sign SILLY and then warn everyone that they may feel that way while learning the signs because they will be using their hands and faces in ways they aren't used to. We always feel silly when we're learning something new, I tell them, and I invite everyone to sign SILLY while making their silliest faces. This gets people laughing and loosened up and establishes both an expectation and a comfort level from the start.

Demonstrating the Signs

The first question many people ask is "Which hand do I use?" For a sign that is performed using only one hand (e.g., any of the manual letters, ELEPHANT, LIBRARY), use your dominant hand. If both hands move during the production of the sign (e.g., BOOK, TIGER), the hands will always move in parallel motion. If one hand moves during the production of a two-handed sign (e.g., READ, SHARE), the hand that moves should always be your dominant hand, and the stationary hand will always be your nondominant hand. If you are right-handed, your right hand is your dominant hand. For lefties, the left hand is dominant.

At the beginning of your program, you may need to tell people that it's okay to copy the signs as you make them. This is especially true with younger groups. Show each sign several times, and monitor the group to make sure everyone is doing it properly. Offer reinforcement ("Great facial expression!" or "Good job!") often and gentle corrections when necessary ("Put your pinkie up. . . . There you go!"). Be sure to go slowly enough for your audience to keep up.

If you aren't sure how to produce a sign, don't guess, and by all means, *don't* make one up. (That would be like saying, "Well, it sort of sounds like French . . . close enough.") Check with a resource person who knows ASL, or consult ASL videos or dictionaries. Many dictionaries include a narrative description of the sign production that can help illuminate the pictures. While dictionaries are not a good method for learning signs initially, they can be a valuable resource for helping you remember signs you've learned before.

When introducing signs, don't always speak the English equivalent of the sign. The ideal way to learn ASL is to disconnect from English altogether and learn each sign in context to associate it with the meaning, not with the English equivalent. (Not all signs even *have* an exact English equivalent.) This is why most ASL classes are taught entirely voices-off. In a storytime situation, it's probably not practical to introduce every sign this way, but you can vary your approach. You can use visual elements such as pictures, puppets, and actions to demonstrate the meanings of signs. You can also invite participants to guess the meanings of signs from context. For example, you might say, "Little Miss Muffet sat on a tuffet, eating some curds and whey. Along came a . . ." and sign SPIDER. Even small children will understand the signs if presented in this fashion.

Sharing American Sign Language

Don't be afraid to share the things you've learned with kids, no matter what age group you decide to focus on. Even if you're not an expert at the language, you *are* an expert at programming for and informing and entertaining kids. Use the skills you already have, add in some ASL, present the whole thing with enthusiasm and a "let's learn together" attitude, and you'll have programs that can't miss!

CHAPTER SIX

Reaching Out

Science may have found a cure for most evils; but it has found no remedy for the worst of them all—the apathy of human beings.

—Helen Keller

So far, we've been focusing on the individual librarian as the one who develops and presents programs relating to sign language. But you don't have to do it alone! Using resources from your community can allow you to present diverse programs incorporating American Sign Language, while minimizing time and effort on your part. Even if you *do* decide to develop and present these programs yourself, making use of outside staff, volunteers, and community groups can support and enrich your programs even further. This chapter offers suggestions for enlisting aid from your community. You can then share the suggestions and sample programs in this book with your new helpers.

Grow Your Own Support Staff

If you look, you may find the ideal person to help you offer sign language programs right on your own staff. With more and more libraries encouraging, or even requiring, cross-training of all staff, incorporating sign language into storytimes offers an ideal way to include adult or circulation department staff members in programming. Many of those who don't choose children's librarianship feel uncomfortable presenting programs, especially initially. Giving these staff members responsibility for only a part of the program—learning and presenting a few signs—provides a gentle introduction to storytime.

Start out by polling members of the other departments to see who might have an interest in partnering with you for sign language storytimes. Emphasize that extensive background isn't necessary, just a willingness to learn and share the signs. If someone on your staff already knows ASL or has deaf family members, so much the better! Point your new partner toward the relevant parts of this book, and give him or her a list of specific signs you would like to use in the program.

When working in partnership with another staff member, remember that *you* are the expert in programming. Your partner may be uncomfortable with specific aspects of programming, such as signing or group management. Talk about these issues ahead of time, and practice with your partner until you both feel comfortable. Clarify the roles of each party: Will you present the entire program, with your partner only demonstrating the signs? Or will your partner take responsibility for a specific part, say a fingerplay incorporating some signs? During the program, you will be modeling programming techniques without even realizing it, and your partner will gradually become more familiar with the storytime process. This is also an excellent way to introduce interns or trainees to programming.

When you are looking for staff volunteers, think broadly. Might someone on your administrative staff or maintenance staff be interested in sharing sign language with children? Involving staff from different departments will not only enrich the experience bank of your organization but also create a unique and enhanced program for your patrons.

The Power of Volunteers

Volunteers can assist with incorporating sign language into programs in much the same way staff from other departments can. If you have a regular volunteer who helps out at storytime, approach him or her about learning some signs in preparation for each program. Be sure to share the resources for learning the signs in chapter 2. Survey your current volunteers to see if any of them have an interest. Preparing a short list of signs for a program is a great service project for a teen volunteer or a great learning experience for a volunteer of any age. As always, remember that *you* are the programming expert, and your volunteer will look to you to handle most of the heavy programming. Make sure the volunteer's role and responsibilities are clearly defined.

Another option is to look for a new volunteer, advertising your specific desire to incorporate signs into your programming. Depending on the degree to which you want to incorporate ASL, you may require a certain background knowledge for your volunteers. If you simply want to incorporate four or five signs a week into your regular programs, then sending your volunteer

off with a list of signs and a video from which to learn them might be suffi-
cient. If, however, you'd like to present more in-depth ASL programs but
you lack the confidence or time to prepare, you will find several community
resources you can tap:

Experts. Your community has several places where experts on ASL and
deafness can be found, such as schools for the deaf and community colleges where ASL is taught. Staff at these institutions may be willing to
put together programs, for free or for a small fee, or may be willing to
serve as resource people for you. Even if the staff members are unwilling
to volunteer their time for the library, it's likely that the librarian or
secretary at your local school for the deaf will be able to put you in
contact with other resource people in your community. Public schools
in your community may also offer ASL classes—more and more high
schools do so these days—and so the teachers there may be able to
assist you as well.

You may also want to talk to interpreters in your community to see
if you can find a programmer there. Beware, though, that fluency in
ASL and an ability to interpret does not necessarily translate into an
ability to teach and present, and some interpreters may feel uncomfortable presenting themselves as experts on ASL at the expense of deaf
people who use ASL as their native language.

Don't hesitate to ask deaf people to present programs relating to sign
language. ASL is, after all, their native language, and so a deaf presenter is often the ideal person to teach basic ASL to your patrons.
Your library may or may not need to provide a voice interpreter,
depending on the kind of program being presented. The deaf presenter
may prefer to give a program *without* voice interpretation so that the
hearing people can learn signs without connecting them to speech.
Discuss the details of the program with your presenter, and clarify such
needs well in advance.

Parents. Odds are you already know several parents who use baby signs
with their infants and toddlers. Why not ask one or two of them to
develop a program about the topic, drawing from their own personal
experiences? They could either put something together themselves or
partner with you to develop a developmentally appropriate baby storytime incorporating signs for babies and information for parents.

Students. Community college or high school students in sign language
classes might be the most eager programming assistants you could ever
find. Though their knowledge may be basic, it is usually enough to

incorporate some simple signs into programs, and these students have the benefit of having studied background information about ASL as well. Again, make sure that you clarify the volunteer's role in the program and give specific guidelines about how the signs will be incorporated.

Partnering with Community Groups

The volunteers to be found in community groups fall into all of the categories mentioned already, from experts to students, but partnering with a group gives you the advantage of an organized approach and a deeper connection to your community. Many groups are eager to take on service projects—why not contact one of the groups in the following list and suggest they develop a sign language program or assist in your development of one? How in-depth the program would be depends on your needs and their knowledge. Use your judgment and creativity when working out the details with these groups.

College sign language or interpreting clubs. Most schools that offer deaf studies or interpreter preparation programs will have a club of this kind, and most are eager to share sign language with the community. Some schools even support voices-off dormitories or houses, where the students experience complete immersion in ASL. Invite members to come and talk about their experiences and share some signs with your audience.

Local schools for the deaf. Deaf kids love to share what they know, just like hearing kids. Why not arrange for a group of middle or high schoolers from your local school for the deaf to come share stories and signs with your patrons? It's sure to be a memorable experience for all involved.

State associations of the deaf. Your state association of the deaf will be a tremendous resource for finding experts to present on just about any topic relating to deafness and ASL, particularly for more in-depth presentations.

Scouting groups. Many Scout groups and other groups of this type take on service projects, and some may even be able to incorporate learning signs into badge projects. Contact your local Scout leader and explain what you'd like to do, and then brainstorm ways the group could get involved. Putting together a storytime using sign language, in which each group member takes a part, would be a great project. The final presentation is guaranteed to draw parents and siblings of the presenters as well as members of your community interested in sign language—and may even garner some publicity for your library as well.

Treat Your Partners Well

Partnerships are an excellent way to increase your library's standing in the community, and sign language programs are a relatively easy way to create partnerships. Many partnerships fail because they lack clearly defined roles and specific tasks. Asking a group to present a program or help you develop one puts clear expectations on the table and offers clear measures for success in the attendance of the programs. No matter whom you partner with, make sure you offer something in return—the best partnerships, after all, are those in which both parties benefit. Whether you can provide service learning hours, assistance in achieving a Scout badge, or greater exposure for a community group, be sure to emphasize the things the library can offer.

Growing Your Own Group

As we have seen, teens are often voracious learners of sign language. If you offer programs, either alone or with help, for this age group, odds are you will see many of the same faces again and again. Consider approaching these students to present or help you present programs for younger children about sign language. They will no doubt be thrilled to share their newfound knowledge. You might even consider developing a kind of teen advisory board or sign language club in your library, which would meet regularly to learn more signs and develop programs for younger children. Guide the development of the programs using your knowledge and expertise, but make sure to let the teens brainstorm the ideas and themes and take the lead in sharing the signs and stories.

No matter how you incorporate other people's talents in your programs, they are sure to enrich the experience for everyone involved!

CHAPTER SEVEN

Drawing Them In

[My mother] never let me use my deafness as an excuse. We had a positive
environment, where if you fail, just try again.

—Heather Whitestone, 1995 Miss America

So far we've focused on how to incorporate sign language into your programs—but all that work won't matter a bit if you can't get people in the
door. While using ASL in your programs may provide a draw in itself, it's up
to you to get the word out about your newly enhanced programs. This chapter offers tips for marketing your programs to both deaf and hearing audiences.

Bring Your Collection Up to Date

It's a given that your programming is expected to support circulation. Something as simple as setting up a display of library materials in your storytime
room can impact circulation statistics. You will most likely find that programs incorporating ASL generate even more check-outs from these in-room
displays than most other programs if the materials you showcase are topical
and age appropriate; once you spark an interest in sign language by using it
in your programs, attendees will be eager to learn more.

Unfortunately, many libraries' collections of sign language materials are
worn, unappealing, or just plain outdated. As you start to look for materials
to supplement your programs, you will probably find this yourself—imagine
how it would look to patrons to set up a display full of such books and videos.
Because of the myriad misconceptions about deafness and ASL that have
been discussed throughout this book, many of the books and videotapes pro-

duced by even normally reputable companies are full of creeping inaccuracies.

What's a librarian to do? Fortunately, increased knowledge about the deaf community and its language means that more and more solid ASL materials are being produced. Also, more resources are available now than have ever been available in the past to help you find the best sign language materials for your collection.

First, evaluate your current sign language materials using the following criteria:

Date. How old are the materials? Be leery of anything more than ten years old because it may promote old-fashioned ideas. Watch for outdated terms such as *Ameslan* (a term used for ASL in the 1970s and 1980s). Some items, of course, are classics—if you find an older item included on one of the recommended lists in this book, it's safe to keep it in your collection.

Format. Remember that ASL is a three-dimensional, visual language and is therefore better learned from videotapes than from books. Is a significant portion of your sign language materials in video or DVD format, or do you have only books in your collection?

Language. In chapter 3, we briefly discussed the differences between ASL and Signed English. Many older sign language materials use Signed English exclusively—a good way to check for this is to flip through the books and see how they represent sentences. If a book shows sign equivalents for every word in an English sentence, including *is* and *are*, and shows them in English word order, then the book is using Signed English, *not* ASL. It may be perfectly appropriate to have some Signed English materials in your collection; just make sure that they don't outnumber the ASL materials, and make sure these items are clearly labeled as using Signed English. Some older books make no differentiation between the two—or worse, claim to teach ASL when they are really showing Signed English.

Variety of target ages. Are your sign language materials top or bottom heavy? Do you have twenty books in your children's department but only a few in adult? Are baby signs represented? Evaluate the breadth of your collection to make sure you have items for all age groups that will be looking for them.

Cultural information. Too many sign language books and videos give only laundry lists of vocabulary, without any understanding of the culture behind the language or even that they are *portraying* a language. Some don't even mention deaf people or deafness at all! Make sure deafness and Deaf Culture are represented in your collection.

Credentials of authors and producers. Look at the background information given in author biographies or on the backs of video cases. Were deaf people involved in the production? Lack of involvement by deaf people often leads to perpetuation of misconceptions.

Use your knowledge of manufacturers' backgrounds to evaluate the work as well. A video produced by Gallaudet University, for example, is far more likely to contain accurate information than one produced by a mainstream company with no connection to deafness, no matter how slick the latter may look to outsiders. Don't limit yourself to big-budget mainstream books and productions—some of the best ASL materials today are being produced by small low-budget companies who have a passion for sharing the language. See the resources in the next section for information on how to find these gems.

Visual quality. Are the signs easy to understand? If the item is a book, are the movements of the signs depicted clearly? Are written explanations of the signs included? Most of all, is the item visually appealing?

Recommended Resources

In addition to the bibliographies of recommended materials in this book, you can find detailed lists of recommended books, videos, and other materials relating to ASL at the following websites:

ASL Access (www.aslaccess.org). This organization's site features video reviews by evaluators well versed in ASL and Deaf Culture. ASL Access has created relationships with distributors of sign language videos and so can offer reviews of mainstream productions as well as materials that may never find their way into major review journals. The website also offers a comprehensive listing of video distributors and publishers of sign language books, with detailed contact information.

Laurent Clerc National Deaf Education Center (http://clerccenter.gallaudet.edu/InfoToGo/503.html). The center offers many valuable resources on deafness and sign language, including a list of best sign language books for young readers.

Update Your Collection in One Fell Swoop

A more drastic way to update your collection is to purchase the ASL Access collection of videos. This nonprofit organization's mission is to assist libraries in acquiring a collection of more than two hundred American Sign Language videos. ASL Access works with knowledgeable deaf and hearing evaluators to select the videos, which represent everything from basic ASL instruction to resources for interpreters to stories and poetry in ASL. The organization charges no fee for its services in ordering and shipping the videos, or for the custom flyers and guidebooks it provides. The collection is ideal for a library committed to increasing its ASL collection and can be funded by grants. For more information, see www.aslaccess.org.

Marketing Your Programs to a Hearing Audience

Now that you've got an up-to-date collection and lots of great programs, how do you get those hearing people in the door? First, identify the audience(s) you'd like to target. If you've done this already when developing your programs, you'll have no trouble. Tailor your publicity to catch the interest of this audience. For example, if your target audience is families with young children, then your program write-ups might emphasize the educational benefits of using sign language with babies and toddlers. To target teens, you might mention the excitement of learning about a new language and culture. Make sure that program titles clearly mention sign language if that is a primary focus of the program. (I learned this lesson the hard way when my "What's Your Sign?" program for teens attracted kids interested in astrology, despite my carefully worded description!)

No matter how much you publicize your programs, don't be surprised if initial attendance is low, especially for teen programs. Participants in sign language programs are a notoriously small but dedicated group. Odds are, if you offer these programs consistently, the attendance will grow as word gets out, and you will see many of the same faces appearing again and again.

If you decide to use the techniques in chapter 4, and consistently incorporate a few signs into your regular storytimes, you may decide that it's unnecessary to advertise at all. In this situation, word is likely to spread among interested parents regardless. You may, however, want to mention the extra benefit of sign language in your program publicity.

Be careful not to set up an expectation of in-depth sign language classes. Cautious wording such as "stories, songs, and a sprinkling of sign language" will guard against this. Be honest when writing program publicity; don't set yourself up as an expert if you're not. Wording such as "let's explore sign language together" can save you a lot of headaches. Of course, if you *do* have credentials, or your guest speaker does, milk them for all they're worth!

Consider marketing your sign language programs to local schools and homeschoolers' groups. You might also want to send special notices to moms' clubs and Scout troops to let them know what you're planning.

Reaching a Deaf Audience

Often libraries, theaters, and other cultural organizations will hire interpreters, advertise an interpreted performance or program, and then wonder why deaf people aren't coming in droves. The fact is, it takes a lot more than just providing interpretation to reach a deaf audience. Think about it—do you go to every program presented in English simply because it's your native language?

The most important factor in attracting a deaf audience is carefully choosing which programs to provide interpretation for and to market to the deaf community. Some programs are just inherently less interesting to deaf people in general than are others. The best way to find out which programs will appeal to the deaf people in your area is to ask them. Partner with your local association of the deaf, school for the deaf, or state office on deafness to survey deaf people and find out what kinds of programs would catch their interest. Ask deaf patrons to advise you.

Make sure you also advertise collections of interest to deaf people. Many deaf people are not frequent library users because they have found little in their public libraries that they need. If you have a collection (such as the ASL Access collection mentioned previously), promote it heavily to the deaf community. Plan events around it, and invite the deaf community to participate.

If you are incorporating sign language into your regular storytimes, or even offering programs focusing on basic American Sign Language, don't automatically assume that these will be of interest to deaf folks. (Would you go to a basic English tutorial?) These types of programs will often draw hearing parents with deaf children as well as deaf parents with hearing children, all of whom want to expose their children more to ASL. You may also draw nonsigning deaf people who want to learn the language. But the primary audience for such programs is hearing families who know little or nothing about ASL.

A sure-fire way to draw in a deaf audience is to invite deaf people to present programs. Topics related to ASL and deafness are a natural choice, but don't forget that deaf people are people first and have a variety of backgrounds, talents, and skills to share. Why not invite a deaf lawyer or stockbroker to come and talk about his or her work? How about a deaf teacher during American Education Week? Think creatively, and don't let preconceptions of deafness limit you. Such a speaker is sure to draw interest from the hearing people in your community and will certainly attract deaf people as well. Don't forget, of course, that you will most likely have to provide a voice interpreter. Make sure to clarify such needs with the presenter far in advance of the program.

Marketing to a Deaf Audience

Once you have gotten feedback from deaf people and decided which programs you want to target, you need to develop an effective marketing strategy. This can be as simple as getting the information about your program into the hands of organizations that can spread the word to deaf people. Contact your local or state school for the deaf—and remember that most residential schools serve an entire state, so even if they are not located close to your library, they may serve families who are. Many schools publish monthly newsletters for families and would be glad to include information about your programs. Your state association for the deaf or office on deafness can also be an invaluable resource, both for spreading the word about your programs and for pointing you to additional groups and outlets for your publicity.

Never underestimate the power of word of mouth—or, in this case, word of hand. Like all small communities, the deaf community has a tremendously efficient grapevine. If you involve deaf people in the planning and presentation of your programs, you can be sure that they will spread the word too.

And of course, any program you want to market to the deaf community will need to be interpreted. Your library should have a policy in place about providing interpreters on request, as required by the Americans with Disabilities Act, but for programs that you specifically market to deaf people, it's good form to advertise that an interpreter will be provided, with no special request necessary. We now turn to the issue of hiring interpreters for programs.

What Interpreters Do

Many people think that the interpreter simply shows up, conveys information from one language to another, and then goes home. In reality, it's a much more complicated process than that. Interpreting requires years of training and practice, and just because someone is a skilled signer, that doesn't mean that he or she has interpreting skills. A variety of factors influence every interpreting situation, including setting, number of deaf and hearing participants, languages involved, lighting, sight lines, sound systems, and content.

Knowing how to work with interpreters will help you provide the best possible service to both your deaf and hearing patrons. First, be aware that there are many different kinds of interpreting, including ASL, Signed English, oral interpreting (for people who speechread), and deaf-blind interpreting. Make sure you state clearly in your publicity which kind of interpreting will be provided, and let people know what to do for other special needs. Most interpreted programs will include ASL interpretation (and indeed, if you state generically that "interpretation will be provided," most deaf people will assume it to be ASL). But understand that this may not fulfill everyone's needs, particularly for deaf-blind individuals. A statement such as the following will ensure that everyone feels welcome: "American Sign Language interpretation will be provided. If you require another accommodation for a special need, please contact . . ."

And of course, for programs presented by deaf presenters, make sure to clarify whether voice interpretation will be provided.

Procuring Interpreters
Whether you are looking for interpreters for a one-time program or filling a patron request, strive to have a system in place in your library. It will make everyone's lives easier and will avoid irritation for deaf patrons when they request interpreters (they won't have to watch the staff scuttle around wondering what to do). The policy should include guidelines for how far in advance the interpreter should be requested (two weeks is fairly standard), how the staff member taking the request moves it into the system, how the interpreter is hired, and where the payment for the interpreter will come from. Some organizations are reluctant to pay for interpreters—if you run into resistance, remind other people in your library that, as a public agency, you are required by law to provide interpreters on request. Also be careful about where the money to pay interpreters comes from—I know a librarian who struggled for years to come up with money for interpreters from her minuscule programming budget, only to find that the payment was supposed to be coming from personnel funds.

Interpreters *can* be expensive, no doubt; they are trained professionals providing a valuable service. Standard payment for an interpreter can run anywhere from $25 per hour to $40 per hour, depending on your location, the interpreting situation, and whether or not the interpreter is nationally certified. A two-hour minimum payment for any interpreting job is standard in the industry.

One way to make booking interpreters easier for your organization is to work through an interpreting agency. There are many benefits to working through an agency: the agency does all the legwork for you in finding the interpreter(s), the agency provides the interpreter with needed information, and you can be assured that the interpreter has been through the agency's screening process. Of course, these services also carry a cost in addition to the interpreter's fee. If your library works under a state or county government, find out how that overarching organization handles booking interpreters; it may have an existing contract with an agency that you can piggyback on.

Many libraries develop their own lists of freelance interpreters, whom they call on whenever they have a need. This method can save you money because you will be paying only the interpreter and not an agency, but it can also be time consuming. Many freelance interpreters are busy people, particularly during the day, and so may be unavailable when you need them. In addition, unless the interpreters on your list are nationally certified, you have no way of knowing their skill levels or experience. (And nationally certified interpreters may be unwilling to take on jobs in libraries, where the pay is generally less than they can make elsewhere.)

Be aware that certification, while highly desirable, is not necessarily needed for most of the interpreting situations found in libraries. Many highly skilled and experienced interpreters have never gone for the national certification test, which is not required to work in the field. Depending on the kind of program for which you need interpreters, you might even be able to recruit students doing advanced interpreting work. Most interpreting programs require a practicum or internship component; a student at this stage would certainly be able to handle a children's storytime, especially with time to prepare in advance. Don't, however, use this as a way to "cut costs" and avoid paying interpreters—most interpreting programs have strict guidelines about practicum students taking paid work away from other interpreters. If a college near you offers interpreter training, contact the coordinator and discuss how you might recruit students for your interpreting needs.

Working with an Interpreter

The most important thing to understand when working with an interpreter is that the interpreter is there for both the hearing and the deaf people. After all, if everyone in the situation knew ASL, no interpreter would be necessary. Often, organizations that hire interpreters expect the interpreter to just show up and do the job without "getting in the way."

However, the complex nature of the interpreting process means that things will go a lot more smoothly if you prepare the interpreter ahead of time. Provide as much advance information as possible, including how many people you expect to attend, how many deaf and how many hearing people will be there, age of participants, and the purpose of the program. It's especially important to let the interpreter know what stories or songs you will be using in your program—literature and music are notoriously difficult to interpret, and a good interpreter will want a chance to prepare. If you are the kind of programmer who likes to bring in a variety of materials and decide what to use as you go, you can still provide your interpreter with a list of the materials you might use, along with an explanation of your style.

Lighting and sight lines are two other vital issues you will want to discuss with the interpreter. Work out a place for the interpreter to stand where the deaf participants will be able to see both the presenter and the interpreter without turning their heads too much. Warn the interpreter if you are planning to use any particular visual props so he or she can work the interpretation around them. Lighting is also extremely important—if you are planning to dim the lights in the room for any reason, including to show a video or use an overhead projector, make sure you provide a lamp or other focused lighting for the interpreter.

If your interpreter is going to be voice interpreting for a deaf presenter, you will most likely need to provide a microphone; the interpreter will need to sit facing the presenter and so will have his or her back to the rest of the audience, which may make it difficult for people to hear without a microphone. The interpreter will need time to consult with the deaf presenter before the program as well.

If you are presenting a storytime, the hearing children in the audience will be fascinated with the interpreter. You will probably want to provide a brief explanation of the interpreter's role at the beginning of the program because many children will not have seen an interpreter before. Your explanation could be as simple as "Miss Suzy is an interpreter. When we say something in English, she interprets it into American Sign Language so that our deaf friends know what we're saying. When our deaf friends sign something, Miss Suzy will say it English so we know what they are saying."

Be careful about involving the interpreter too much in your program. It's very awkward for the interpreter to be selected as a volunteer in an activity or used as a character in a story when he or she is trying to do the job of communicating what's happening. Conversely, don't ignore the deaf participants, thinking that the interpreter has them handled. Involve them in the program just as you do the hearing participants. Don't assume that the deaf people can't enjoy the songs, for instance. Set a good example for your participants by speaking directly to the deaf people in your group—don't say, "Tell her I said . . ."

Try to remember that the interpreter will always be a little behind what you are saying. Therefore, when you ask the group a question, the deaf people will not get that information at the same time as the hearing people. This can mean that deaf kids don't get picked to volunteer because they don't raise their hands as quickly as the hearing kids do. Try to be fair, and whenever you ask a question of the group, allow a moment before you choose someone to respond.

A good interpreter will arrive early to go over these and other issues with you. Be prepared to share as much information about your program as you can, and don't be afraid to ask questions. Remember that the interpreter's job is to facilitate communication. But be aware that interpreters follow a code of ethics. If you have questions about the deaf people coming to your program, it's appropriate to pose those questions to the deaf people themselves, *not* to the interpreter, who probably couldn't answer those kinds of questions even if he or she was not bound by confidentiality requirements.

Evaluating Your Programs

Evaluating your programs on a regular basis will help you strengthen them and determine public interest for future programs. There are many ways to evaluate the effectiveness of your programs:

Patron survey. A brief two-question evaluation handed out at the end of a program can give you a valuable sense of patron satisfaction. ("What did you like about this program? What would you change about this program?")

Informal comments. Jot down comments that patrons make as they leave your programs. They will give you helpful ideas for the future, as well as a good sense of how people are responding. Though this kind of survey will not help with formal documentation needs, it can be a valuable source of ongoing internal program evaluation.

Attendance. Attendance is a time-honored means of assessing program effectiveness. Naturally a well-attended program is considered a successful one, but remember that often sign language programs, particularly for teens, take some time to build an audience. Weigh your attendance in the balance with the enthusiasm of those who do attend—and remember that, even if you've only touched four or five

people with your program, that's four or five people who have had their
eyes opened to something they knew little or nothing about before.

Circulation. Also a traditional means of assessing program effectiveness,
circulation can tell you a lot about how well your programs are doing.
Sign language programs are perhaps more likely than most others to
stimulate an interest in the library's collection, so check your circulation statistics periodically to see how ASL materials are moving, and
don't forget to include these numbers in any formal program justifica-
tions you might need to prepare.

Give Yourself a Hand

By doing something as simple as incorporating American Sign Language into
your programs, you have the power to open the minds of children and share
a beautiful, often misunderstood language. You can become a bridge between
hearing and deaf people, simply by having the right attitude and a willing
heart. Every participant who comes to your programs will benefit, and so will
you. You've already taken the vital first step by reading this book and taking
the time to learn about a new culture and a new language. Now go out there
and pass it on.

PART II

PROGRAMS FOR ALL AGES

In this section, you'll find twenty-eight program plans ready for you to use. For each age group (except middle school), samples are provided of programs that incorporate a few signs, as well as several programs that focus more heavily on ASL. Each listing includes a program description, a list of the signs used, a program plan, and a list of supplementary materials on the topic. The list of signs used in each program includes only signs not already illustrated in the recommended books for that program, and all signs listed are found in appendix E. Complete information about books and songs recommended to use with signs is found in appendix B, which gives further suggestions for presenting the song or story, as well as a complete list of signs to use. Books that focus on ASL or deafness are identified with asterisks, and annotations and more information about using these resources in programs is found in appendix A.

The factual information included in the baby-sign programs is taken from *Sign with Your Baby: How to Communicate with Infants before They Can Speak* by Joseph Garcia. For additional information about this book and other resources for planning baby-sign programs, see appendix A. For family programs, book options for older and younger groups are given, with the suggestions for older children always listed first.

Four program plans are provided for middle school programs, each focusing on a different aspect of ASL. These are appropriate to use as stand-alone programs or as part of a series. If you choose to use them as a series, you may wish to add an ongoing project that participants practice each week, such as learning to sign the Pledge of Allegiance.

CHAPTER EIGHT

Baby Programs

Having a Ball

Program description: Roll over to the library for some simple stories, songs, and even some sign language about one of baby's favorite toys.

Signs used in this program: BALL, numbers 1–3

Song: "Clap Along with Me" from *Wee Sing for Baby* by Pamela Conn Beall and Susan Hagen Nipp

Book: *Ball!* by Ros Asquith

Teach sign: BALL (Use sign throughout the following activities.)

Flannelboard rhyme: "Here's a Ball"
   (Model counting in ASL after explaining it to parents.)
   Here's a ball, and here's a ball,
   And here's a ball I see. Shall we count them?
   Are you ready? One . . . two . . . three.

Bounce: "Bouncy Ball"
   My baby's like a bouncy ball,
   Bouncing up and down.
   Baby bounce left, baby bounce right,
   Baby bounce all around!

Action song: "Roll the Ball" (to the tune of "Row Row Row Your Boat")
   (Have the babies and parents sit in a circle. Roll the ball to each child in turn and have him or her roll it back to you.)
   Roll roll roll the ball,
   Roll it here to me.
   And then I roll it back again,
   Quick as one, two, three.

Book: *Pickle and the Ball* by Lynn Breeze

Flannelboard activity: Allow each participant to come up and place a ball on the flannelboard.

Closing song: "Clap Tap Bend" from *It's Toddler Time* by Carol Hammett and Elaine Bueffel

Other materials to use with this theme:

Spot Visits His Grandparents by Eric Hill

Kipper's Lost Ball by Mick Inkpen

Sam's Ball by Barbro Lindgren

The Ball Bounced by Nancy Tafuri

"One Is a Giant" from *The Baby Record* by Bob McGrath and Katharine Smithram

Bathtime Bubbles!

Program description: Soap up those little tummies, and get ready for a bathtime storytime full of surprises! We'll celebrate getting clean with age-appropriate stories, bounces, activities, and even a little sign language.

Signs used in this program: DIRTY, CLEAN

Opening song: "Look at My Hands" from *Signing Time Songs, Volumes 1–3* by Rachel de Azevedo Coleman

Prop story: "Little Monster's Bath"

(Make a posterboard bathtub front from a copier paper box, and gather several animal puppets, as well as a monster or child stuffed toy to play the main character. Use bubbles and a spray bottle full of water when the animals jump into the tub.)

Little Monster was taking a bath. He splashed in the water. He blew bubbles in the air. He played with his toy boat. He loved his bath.

DING-DONG. Little Monster got out of the tub and wrapped his towel around him. He opened the door.

It was a little green frog. "Ribbit! Can I share your bath, Little Monster?"

"Sure!" said Little Monster. The frog hopped into the water with a SPLASH. Little Monster hopped in too. Little Monster and the frog splashed and played.

(Continue the pattern, with the animals growing gradually larger. End with a very large animal, such as an elephant or a bear.)

Little Monster looked at his wonderful bath. Hardly any suds were left. He looked for his toy boat, but he couldn't find it with all the animals in the tub.

"You know what?" he said. "You all have fun. I'm going to go take a shower!"

Song: "Everybody Wash" from *Splish Splash: Bath Time Fun*

Rhyme: "Rub-a-Dub-Dub" (traditional)
Rub-a-dub-dub, three men in a tub,
And who do you think they be?
The butcher, the baker, the candlestick maker,
They all set out to sea!
Bounce: "Rubba-Dubba Duckie"
Rubba-dubba duckie, swimming in my bath.
We wash and we play and we splash splash splash!
My little rubber duckie is oh so funny.
We always laugh when I wash my tummy!
Story: *Clifford Counts Bubbles* by Norman Bridwell
Activity: Blowing Bubbles
Invite participants to pop bubbles as you blow them. Play selections from Joanie Bartels's *Bathtime Magic* or the *Sesame Street* CD *Splish, Splash* in the background.
Song: "Wash Your Head Shoulders Knees and Toes" from *Bathtime Magic* by Joanie Bartels
Other materials to use with this theme:
Clifford's Bathtime by Norman Bridwell
Bathtime for Biscuit by Alyssa Satin Capucilli
Maisy Takes a Bath by Lucy Cousins
Mrs. Wishy-Washy by Joy Cowley
Bathtime edited by Lara Holtz
Splash! by Flora McDonnell
"The Bath" from *Henry and Mudge in the Green Time* by Cynthia Rylant
Splish, Splash by Jeff Sheppard
Max's Bath by Rosemary Wells
"Five Little Ducks" from *Hello Everybody! Playsongs and Rhymes from a Toddler's World* by Rachel Buchman
"This Little Pig Had a Rub a Dub Dub" from *The Baby Record* by Bob McGrath and Katharine Smithram

Baby Signs at Home

Program description: Did you know that babies can sign long before they can speak? It's true! Join us for stories, songs, and signs, and learn more about the benefits of using sign language with babies and toddlers.
Signs used in this program: EAT/FOOD, COW, MILK, CHICKEN, EGG, BEE, HONEY, BREAD, THANK-YOU, PLEASE, SHARE, TURN, APPLE, CRACKER, STAR

Opening song: "Wake Up Toes" from *Morning Magic* by Joanie Bartels

Fact: Children can learn to sign long before they have the ability to speak. Also, children exposed to sign language early in life will not only find it easy to learn ASL later, they will find it easier to learn *any* language later.

Story: *Baby's Breakfast* by Emilie Poulsson (Teach signs for EAT/FOOD and foods in story.)

Fact: Using sign language with your baby can reduce frustration for both of you. Your baby can tell you exactly what he or she wants!

Song: "Magic Words" from *Signing Time Songs, Volumes 1–3* by Rachel de Azevedo Coleman

Book: *Baby's First Signs* by Kim Votry**

Fact: Teach the signs for everyday objects and activities first. Use the objects to reinforce the signs often, until your child begins to sign back. Remember, your child can understand you before he or she signs it back, so keep using it. If the child begins to sign back, reward him or her with lots of smiles and hugs and kisses.

Bounce: Teach signs APPLE, CRACKER

(Do bounce three times at increasing speed.)

Lunchtime is my favorite time

Because I love to eat!

I eat some apples and some crackers

Then drink some juice so sweet!

Fact: Reinforce signs throughout the day to help you both remember them. You can learn signs from books, though videos and live people are usually a lot easier. *Signing Time!* is a great series of videos and DVDs to help you learn to sign with your baby.

Fact: When using signs with your baby, it's a good idea to use American Sign Language. There's a big difference between American Sign Language, which is a whole language, and Signed English, which is just a manual code to represent English words. If you use ASL, you're giving your child (and yourself) a chance to become bilingual. And remember, ASL is a language that has a whole culture attached to it, so it's a good idea to learn a little bit about the language before you start using it.

Activity: Blowing Bubbles

Fact: Some people worry that using sign language impairs children's ability to learn speech. Not true. Actually, it *increases* their speech abilities later because it stimulates the language centers of the brain and encourages those neural pathways to become stronger. There has also been a lot of research in recent years that sign language can help hearing children learn to read by giving an additional avenue to language.

Teach signs: STAR

Song: "Twinkle Twinkle Little Star" with sign

Fact: Sign language is not only good for your baby, it's also fun! And it's not just for babies either—keep up the learning as your child begins to speak, and you and your child can develop a second language together. Check out the informative handout I have prepared for resources to continue your learning together. Now it is time to bring out our toys for an informal playtime. While the babies are playing, I will be around to pass out the handout and answer any questions you might have. Before that, though, I have one more important sign to show you. THANK-YOU for coming!

Other materials to use with this theme:

Nicky and Grandpa by Cathryn Falwell

Spot Bakes a Cake by Eric Hill

Baby Loves by Michael Lawrence

Baby Loves Hugs and Kisses by Michael Lawrence

I Kissed the Baby by Mary Murphy

Family by Helen Oxenbury

Toby Counts His Marbles by Cyndy Szekeres

Tickle Tum! by Nancy Van Laan

"The Family" from *Wee Sing for Baby* by Pamela Conn Beall and Susan Hagen Nipp

"This Is What I See" from *Hello Everybody! Playsongs and Rhymes from a Toddler's World* by Rachel Buchman

"Baby a Go Go" from *The Baby Record* by Bob McGrath and Katharine Smithram

"Cluck, Cluck, Red Hen" from *The Corner Grocery Store* by Raffi

Baby Signs at Play

Program description: Learn about the cognitive benefits of using sign language with babies in this interactive program full of age-appropriate signs and activities for babies and fascinating information for parents. You and your baby will have so much fun you won't even realize you're learning!

Signs used in this program: PLAY, CAT, HORSE, COW, DUCK, PIG, DOG, numbers 1–5, THANK-YOU

Opening song: "Head, Shoulders, Knees and Toes" from *It's Toddler Time* by Carol Hammett and Elaine Bueffel

Introduction: Today we're going to share baby signs! Babies have the ability to sign before they can speak, and by sharing signs with your little one now, you can develop his or her language abilities for the future. Your baby can also communicate with you before he or she can speak. Throughout today's program, I'll be sharing some signs with you, along with some tips for using sign language with your baby during playtime.

Story: *I Went Walking* by Sue Williams

Fact: There are lots of places to sign! You can use sign language at home, in the car, at the park, or while reading stories.

Song: "As I Was Walking to Town One Day" from *The Baby Record* by Bob McGrath and Katharine Smithram (Use animal puppets with this song to reinforce the animal signs learned in the previous story.)

Fact: You can sign in different places too: on yourself, on your baby, on a stuffed animal, on a book. Each of these ways to sign will reinforce the concept in your baby's mind.

Bounce: Here we go up up up.
Here we go down down down.
Here we go all around!

Fact: Don't always say the word at the same time that you make the sign. Vary the visual and aural stimulation to encourage your child to use different senses.

Song: "Hickory Dickory Dock" from *Wee Sing for Baby* by Pamela Conn Beall and Susan Hagen Nipp

Fact: Give your baby lots of praise every time he or she signs back to you. This will encourage your baby to keep trying!

Story: *Pickle and the Blocks* by Lynn Breeze

Fact: Your baby won't always sign the signs correctly at first. Praise him or her anyway. Keep signing the correct way, and eventually your baby will also do it right.

Flannelboard: Counting Blocks
Baby loves to play with blocks.
I see a red block
and a yellow block
and a green block
and a blue block
and an orange block
Can you help me count them?
One, two, three, four, five.
Let's build them way up high
and then knock them down! Wheee!

Fact: Did you know that a typical nine-month-old can understand only about ten words of spoken language but can develop a vocabulary of about seventy-five signs?

Song: "Bumping Up and Down" from *Singable Songs for the Very Young* by Raffi

Fact: Check out the informative handout I have prepared for resources to continue your learning together! Now it is time to bring out our toys for an informal playtime. While the babies are playing, I will be around to pass out the handout and answer any questions you might have. Before that, though, I have one more important sign to show you. THANK-YOU for coming!

Other materials to use with this theme:

Playtime for Zoo Animals by Caroline Arnold

Ball! by Ros Asquith

Pickle and the Ball by Lynn Breeze

Whose Nose and Toes? by John Butler

Nicky's Walk by Cathryn Falwell

Mama Cat Has Three Kittens by Denise Fleming

I Love Animals by Flora McDonnell

It's Spring! by Else Holmelund Minarik

Come Along, Daisy by Jane Simmons

Daisy's Day Out by Jane Simmons

Out for a Walk by Kim Votry**

"I Like to Swing" from *Hello Everybody! Playsongs and Rhymes from a Toddler's World* by Rachel Buchman

"A Tickle Rhyme" from *Hello Everybody! Playsongs and Rhymes from a Toddler's World* by Rachel Buchman

"Jack in the Box" from *It's Toddler Time* by Carol Hammett and Elaine Bueffel

"Rickety Rickety Rocking Horse" from *The Baby Record* by Bob McGrath and Katharine Smithram

"Willoughby Wallaby Woo" from *Singable Songs for the Very Young* by Raffi

"Tommy Thumb" from *Great Big Hits 2* by Sharon, Lois, and Bram

~

CHAPTER NINE

Toddler Programs

Apple of My Eye

Program description: Way up high in the apple tree . . . are a bunch of stories for you and me! Join us for stories, signs, and songs celebrating our favorite treat.

Signs used in this program: Numbers 1–5, APPLE, RED, GREEN, YELLOW

Opening song: "Hello Everybody" from *Hello Everybody! Playsongs and Rhymes from a Toddler's World* by Rachel Buchman

Introduction: Today we are going to listen to stories about apples. This is how you say APPLE (demonstrate sign) in American Sign Language.

Book: *Apple Farmer Annie* by Monica Wellington

Teach signs: RED, YELLOW, GREEN

Flannelboard/magnetboard activity: Sorting Apples

Make three "baskets" like those Annie uses to sort her apples in the previous story. Put a red, yellow, or green stripe on the bottom of each basket. Make enough apples, in red, green, and yellow, so that each child can place one in the correct basket on the flannelboard or magnetboard. Use this activity to reinforce color knowledge and signs.

Book: *The Apple Pie Tree* by Zoe Hall

Teach signs: Numbers 1–5

Action rhyme: "Five Little Apples"

Five little apples hanging in the tree,

And each one said, "You can't get me!"

But I shook and shook and I shook that tree.

Down fell an apple. Crunch! Yummy!

Four little apples . . .

Three little apples . . .
Two little apples . . .
One little apple . . .
Book: *Apples and Pumpkins* by Anne Rockwell
Song: "Shake My Sillies Out" from *More Singable Songs* by Raffi
Other books to use with this theme:
 Ten Red Apples by Virginia Miller
 Apples, Apples, Apples by Nancy Elizabeth Wallace
 "Little Green Apple" from *It's Toddler Time* by Carol Hammett and Elaine
  Bueffel
 "Five Green Apples" from *Mainly Mother Goose* by Sharon, Lois, and
  Bram

In My Garden

Program description: Worms wiggle, children giggle, and flowers bloom
down in the garden! Join us for stories, songs, signs, and rhymes about
things that grow.
Signs used in this program: FLOWER, BEE, CATERPILLAR, numbers 1–5
Opening song: "Round and Round We Go" from *It's Toddler Time* by Carol
Hammett and Elaine Bueffel
Story: *Jasper's Beanstalk* by Nick Butterworth
Dramatic play activity: Grow like a beanstalk.
Song: "The Eensy Weensy Spider" from *Mainly Mother Goose* by Sharon,
Lois, and Bram
Book or flannelboard story: *The Very Hungry Caterpillar* by Eric Carle
Action rhyme: "Bumblebee"
 (Teach the sign BEE and encourage children to sign it during the rhyme.
 When the bee is flying away, show its flight with your thumb and index
 finger.)
 Bumblebee, bumblebee,
 buzz yourself away from me.
 Bzzzzzzzzzzzzzz you say
 as you go along your way.
Flannelboard: "Five Little Flowers"
 (Teach FLOWER and numbers 1–5 to use during this rhyme.)
 Five little flowers grew by my door;
 I picked one for my mother, and then there were four.
 Four little flowers pretty as can be;
 I picked one for my father, and then there were three.

Three little flowers, what could I do?
I picked one for my sister, and then there were two.
Two little flowers out in the sun;
I picked one for my brother, and then there was one.
One little flower, isn't this fun?
I picked one for you, and then there were none.

Book: *I Spy in the Garden* by Richard Powell
Closing song: "In My Garden" from *One Light, One Sun* by Raffi
Other recommended activities for this theme:

Fran's Flower by Lisa Bruce
Rosie's Roses by Pamela Duncan Edwards
Muncha Muncha Muncha by Candace Fleming
Flora's Surprise by Debi Gliori
Ten Rosy Roses by Eve Merriam
"Round and Round the Garden" from *Wee Sing for Baby* by Pamela Conn Beall and Susan Hagen Nipp
"A Tickle Rhyme" from *Hello Everybody! Playsongs and Rhymes from a Toddler's World* by Rachel Buchman
"Here Is a Beehive" from *Sing a Song of Seasons* by Rachel Buchman
"Butterfly" from *It's Toddler Time* by Carol Hammett and Elaine Bueffel
"Spider on the Floor" from *Singable Songs for the Very Young* by Raffi

Sign Language Rainbow

Program description: Red, yellow, green, and blue, have we got a storytime for you! Come and learn basic color signs through stories, songs, and fun activities.

Signs used in this program: RED, ORANGE, YELLOW, GREEN, BLUE, PURPLE, PINK, BLACK, numbers 1–5, RAINBOW

Opening song: "Katie Has a Red Shirt On" (to the tune of "Mary Had a Little Lamb")

Greet participants by naming the color of something each is wearing. Example:

"Katie has a red shirt on, red shirt on, red shirt on.
Katie has a red shirt on, I see her here today."

Make sure to use a verse for each child. To encourage parents to sing along, announce the child's name and the article of clothing and color before beginning to sing. Sign the colors as you sing.

Flannelboard activity: Using a simple flannelboard rainbow, introduce the color signs.

Book or flannelboard story: *Brown Bear, Brown Bear, What Do You See?* by Bill Martin

Flannelboard: Colors in the Rain

(Use color and number signs as you present this activity.)

I took a walk out in the rain

and saw umbrella colors.

What colors do you see?

Orange, blue, green, yellow, and red!

Can you count them? One, two, three, four, five!

Book: *Yellow Umbrella* by Jae Soo Liu

Song: "Baa Baa Black Sheep" (traditional)

For a twist on the old classic, repeat the song with different colored sheep. Use flannelboard pieces or large stick puppets to reinforce the sheep colors.

Baa baa ———— sheep, have you any wool?

Yes sir, yes sir, three bags full.

One for my master, one for my dame,

And one for the little boy who lives down the lane.

Book: *I Love Colors* by Margaret Miller

Closing song: "A Rainbow of Colors" from *We All Live Together, Volume 5* by Greg and Steve

Other materials to use with this theme:

Duckie's Rainbow by Francis Barry

My World of Color by Margaret Wise Brown

Cat's Colors by Jane Cabrera

One Red Rooster by Kathleen Sullivan Carroll

Maisy Goes Swimming by Lucy Cousins

Maisy's Rainbow Dream by Lucy Cousins

Rosie's Roses by Pamela Duncan Edwards

Nicky's Walk by Cathryn Falwell

Mr. Panda's Painting by Anne Rockwell

Who Said Red? by Mary Serfozo

Caps for Sale by Esphyr Slobodkina

Carlo Likes Colors by Jessica Spanyol

Toby Counts His Marbles by Cyndy Szekeres

Mouse's First Summer by Lauren Thompson

Mouse Paint by Ellen Stoll Walsh

Sign Language on the Farm

Program description: Cows are mooing, ducks are quacking, and it's time to learn sign language down on the farm! Join us for stories, songs, and more that teach basic American Sign Language for little ones and grown-ups.

Signs used in this program: GOAT, BIRD, HORSE, COW, DUCK, TURKEY, DOG, PIG, CAT, QUIET, CHICKEN, SHEEP, numbers 1–6, RABBIT, MOTHER, FATHER

Opening song: "Time to Sing" from *One Light, One Sun* by Raffi

Introduction: Today we're going to learn signs for our favorite farm animals. We'll be learning American Sign Language, which is a different language from English. Don't worry if the children don't do the signs correctly right away—we'll be using them again and again, so they will eventually pick them up!

Book: *Down on the Farm* by Merrily Kutner (Teach animal signs as you read the story.)

Song: "Down on the Farm" from *We All Live Together, Volume 5* by Greg and Steve

Action rhyme: "The Cow"

I'd like to be a cow.

I wouldn't have much to do.

I'd stand around the fields all day,

And sometimes I'd say MOOOO.

Book: *Noisy Barn!* by Harriet Ziefert

Song: "Down on Grandpa's Farm" from *One Light, One Sun* by Raffi

Book: *Spot Goes to the Farm* by Eric Hill

Flannelboard song or rhyme: "Six Little Ducks" from *More Singable Songs* by Raffi

Song: "Old MacDonald" from *Jump Up and Sing: Binyah's Favorite Songs*

Other materials to use with this theme:

Little Rabbits' First Farm Book by Alan Baker

Old MacDonald Had a Farm by Holly Berry

In the Spring by Craig Brown

Mr. Gumpy's Motor Car by John Burningham

Whose Nose and Toes? by John Butler

Do You Want to Be My Friend? by Eric Carle

Mrs. Wishy-Washy by Joy Cowley

Mama Cat Has Three Kittens by Denise Fleming

Time for Bed by Mem Fox

The Seals on the Bus by Lenny Hort

I Love Animals by Flora McDonnell

I Kissed the Baby by Mary Murphy

Toddlerobics: Animal Fun by Zita Newcome

It's My Birthday by Helen Oxenbury

Come Along, Daisy by Jane Simmons

Daisy's Day Out by Jane Simmons

This Is the Farmer by Nancy Tafuri

Splish, Splash by Jeff Sheppard

Minerva Louise at School by Janet Morgan Stoeke

Little Quack by Lauren Thompson

Dinnertime! by Sue Williams

I Went Walking by Sue Williams

I Swapped My Dog by Harriet Ziefert

"Five Little Ducks" from *Hello Everybody! Playsongs and Rhymes from a Toddler's World* by Rachel Buchman

"I Had a Little Rooster" from *Hello Everybody! Playsongs and Rhymes from a Toddler's World* by Rachel Buchman

"Old MacDonald Had a Farm" from *Old MacDonald Had a Farm* by the Countdown Kids

"The Farmer in the Dell" from *Old MacDonald Had a Farm* by the Countdown Kids

"Cluck, Cluck, Red Hen" from *The Corner Grocery Store* by Raffi

CHAPTER TEN

Preschool Programs

Happy Valentine's Day!

Program description: Roses are red, violets are blue, our Valentine storytime will be fun for you!

Signs used in this program: SUN, RAIN, I-LOVE-YOU, NO (NONE), numbers 1–5

Introduction: Today we are going to listen to stories about Valentine's Day. This is how you say I-LOVE-YOU (demonstrate sign) in American Sign Language. Many deaf people use American Sign Language to communicate. Do you know what *deaf* means? . . . Right, it means someone who can't hear. Well, I can hear, but I really like American Sign Language, so today we will be learning a little bit of it in our storytime.

Song: "If You're Happy and You Know It" from *Children's Favorite Songs 3* by Larry Groce and the Disneyland Children's Sing-Along Chorus

Book: *Valentine's Day* by Anne Rockwell

Teach signs: Numbers 1–5, NO (NONE)

Flannelboard rhyme: "Five Little Valentines"

Five little valentines sitting by my door;
I gave one to my mother, and then there were four.
Four little valentines so pretty to see;
I gave one to my father, and then there were three.
Three little valentines so shiny and new;
I gave one to my sister, and then there were two.
Two little valentines, isn't this fun?
I gave one to my brother, and then there was one.
One little valentine, and now we're almost done;
I gave one to you, and then there were none!

Book: *One Zillion Valentines* by Frank Modell
Matching activity/rhyme: Use Your Eyes

(Make about forty hearts out of construction paper, and draw designs on them so that each has a match. Use the valentines in *One Zillion Valentines* as inspiration for your designs. Place these hearts on the flannelboard or tape them to a wall in your storytime room, and chant the rhyme below while allowing each child to take a turn to find two hearts that match. This activity is also ideal for pointing out the importance of eyes and seeing in sign language.)

Use your eyes to see the hearts, with many patterns and designs.

Do you see two that go together? ———, show me a match that you can find!

Book: *Clifford's First Valentine's Day* by Norman Bridwell
Teach signs: SUN, RAIN
Song: "You Are My Sunshine" using signs for this program
Other materials to use with this theme:

Ten Rosy Roses by Eve Merriam

Little Bear's Valentine by Else Holmelund Minarik

My Funny Valentine by Harriet Ziefert

I-L-Y Stick Puppets craft (see appendix C)

Wonderful Weather

Program description: Help us celebrate rainy and sunny days through stories, songs, and even some sign language.

Signs used in this program: RAIN, SUN, RAINBOW, numbers 1–5

Introduction: Today we are going to listen to stories about weather. This is how you say RAIN (demonstrate sign) in American Sign Language. Many deaf people use American Sign Language to communicate. Do you know what *deaf* means? . . . Right, it means someone who can't hear. Well, I can hear, but I really like American Sign Language, so today we will be learning a little bit of it in our storytime. Now let's learn about some other kinds of weather. Here's how you sign SUN. (Demonstrate sign.) Are you ready to sing and sign a song about weather?

Song: "If It's Raining and You Know It" (to the tune of "If You're Happy and You Know It")

If it's raining and you know it, hold up your umbrella. . . .

If it's sunny and you know it, put on your sunblock. . . .

Book: *In the Rain with Baby Duck* by Amy Hest

Song: "The Eensy Weensy Spider" from *Mainly Mother Goose* by Sharon, Lois, and Bram

Prop story: *Rainy Day* by Janet Morgan Stoeke

Flannelboard: Colors in the Rain

(Use number signs as you present this activity.)

I took a walk out in the rain

and saw umbrella colors.

What colors do you see?

Orange, blue, green, yellow, and red!

Can you count them? One, two, three, four, five!

Activity: Making a Rainstorm

Divide the room into three groups. Tell the children to watch you and copy what you do as you pass in front of their groups. Begin by having the first group rub their hands together. Add the second and third groups. Then have the first group tap lightly on their legs or the floor. Gradually have the second and the third groups switch over to tapping as well. Next, slowly add in each group snapping their fingers. Increase the speed of the finger snapping. Occasionally have a group clap to represent thunder. As the storm gets to its height, have the children stomp their feet on the floor. Finally, have the storm abate by slowing working each group backward through the process: finger snapping, then tapping, then back to rubbing hands together. When done properly, this sounds like an actual thunderstorm!

Teach sign: RAINBOW

Song: "You Are My Sunshine"

Book: *Kipper's Sunny Day* by Mick Inkpen

Song: "Shake Your Sillies Out" from *More Singable Songs* by Raffi

Other materials to use with this theme:

Rabbits and Raindrops by Jim Arnosky

Mr. Gumpy's Motor Car by John Burningham

Snowballs by Lois Ehlert

A Winter Day by Douglas Florian

What Can You Do in the Rain? by Anna Grossnickle Hines

What Can You Do in the Sun? by Anna Grossnickle Hines

What Can You Do in the Snow? by Anna Grossnickle Hines

What Can You Do in the Wind? by Anna Grossnickle Hines

Kipper's Rainy Day by Mick Inkpen

Kipper's Snowy Day by Mick Inkpen

Cleo in the Snow by Caroline Mockford

Snip, Snip . . . Snow! by Nancy Poydar

The First Snowfall by Anne and Harlow Rockwell
What Will the Weather Be Like Today? by Paul Rogers
Bunny's First Snowflake by Monica Wellington
"Snow Song" from *Hello Everybody! Playsongs and Rhymes from a Toddler's World* by Rachel Buchman
"Mitten Weather" from *Sing a Song of Seasons* by Rachel Buchman
"Let's Play in the Snow" from *Sing a Song of Seasons* by Rachel Buchman
"Over the River and Through the Woods" from *Children's Favorite Songs 3* by Larry Groce and the Disneyland Children's Sing-Along Chorus

Sign Language Friends

Program description: Learn some basic sign language through stories and songs of friendship that remind us how much we all have in common.

Signs used in this program: FRIEND, TOGETHER, SIGN, HAPPY, PIG, HIPPOPOTAMUS, I-LOVE-YOU, YOU, ME, PLEASE, THANK-YOU, TURN, SHARE

Opening song: "The More We Sing Together" from *Kids' Favorite Songs 2*

Introduction: I bet you all have lots of friends. How do you talk to your friends? Do you use words? Today we are going to learn about another way to communicate with our friends: American Sign Language. Do you know what sign language is? It is a language that uses our hands and eyes instead of our mouths and ears. Deaf people use sign language. What does *deaf* mean? It means someone who can't hear. Let me ask you a question: do *only* deaf people use sign language? No! Hearing people can learn it too, and then we can communicate with our deaf friends.

Book: *Too Close Friends* by Shen Roddie

Discussion: The characters in the story were very different, but they were still friends. What are some of the ways you and your friends are different? How are you the same?

Song: "The More We SIGN Together" (Repeat opening song with the following lyrics, signing the words in capital letters.)
The more we SIGN TOGETHER, TOGETHER, TOGETHER,
The more we SIGN TOGETHER, the HAPPIER we'll be.
'Cause your FRIENDS are my FRIENDS,
And my FRIENDS are your FRIENDS.
The more we SIGN TOGETHER, the HAPPIER we'll be.

Book: *Moses Sees a Play* by Isaac Millman**

Dramatic play activity: In the story, Moses and his new friend communicate with each other even though they don't use the same language. Suppose you wanted to tell somebody the story of "Cinderella," like the play that Moses's class sees in the book, but that person didn't know your language. Do you think you could act it out for them, just using your body and no words? Let's act out Cinderella scrubbing the floor. . . . Now let's be the mean stepmother, telling her she can't go to the ball. . . . (Continue through the story, encouraging all the children to act out the different characters with their bodies.)

Song: "Magic Words" from *Signing Time Songs, Volumes 1–3* by Rachel de Azevedo Coleman

Teach sign: I-LOVE-YOU

Closing song: "Friends" (to the tune of "Row Row Row Your Boat")

Here's the sign for YOU, here's the sign for ME.

I hook my fingers together like this 'cause FRIENDS we'll always be!

Other materials to use with this theme:

Mr. Gumpy's Motor Car by John Burningham

Do You Want to Be My Friend? by Eric Carle

David's Drawings by Cathryn Falwell

How I Found a Friend by Irina Hale

What Shall We Play? by Sue Heap

Farfellina and Marcel by Holly Keller

Moses Goes to a Concert by Isaac Millman**

Fall Is for Friends by Suzy Spafford

Where Did Bunny Go? by Nancy Tafuri

I-L-Y Stick Puppets craft (see appendix C)

1–2–3, Sign and Count with Me!

Program description: We're off and counting in American Sign Language! Learn number signs and more through fun stories and songs!

Signs used in this program: TOGETHER, numbers 1–10, MOUSE, SNAKE, HAPPY

Opening song: "We're All Together Again" from *We All Live Together, Volume 5* by Greg and Steve

Introduction: Today we're going to learn about American Sign Language. When we use sign language, do we use our voices and our ears? No, we use our hands and our eyes. Many deaf people use American Sign Language to communicate. *Deaf* means that someone cannot hear. But you can learn sign language whether you can hear or not! Today we're going to learn about numbers in American Sign Language. The numbers might look different from the way you are used to counting on your fingers. That's because, today, we will be counting in another language!

Book: *The Handmade Counting Book* by Laura Rankin** (Use this book to teach the numbers up to ten. The book actually contains higher numbers as well, but you can choose to stop at ten or continue, depending on your audience.)

Song: "The Number Game" from *We All Live Together, Volume 5* by Greg and Steve (reinforces numbers 1–5)

Book: *Mouse Count* by Ellen Stoll Walsh

Flannelboard or prop song: "Roll Over" (traditional)

(Use ten of whatever flannelboard pieces or stuffed animals you have handy for this interactive song—teddy bears, bunnies, even dinosaurs or dragons!)

There were ten in the bed and the little one said, "I'm crowded! Roll over!"

So they all rolled over and one fell out. OUCH!

There were nine in the bed. . .

Song: "This Old Man" from *Old MacDonald Had a Farm* by the Countdown Kids

Transition: When we talk about American Sign Language, many people think of using their hands to communicate, but what else is just as important? When other people talk with their mouths, we listen with our . . . ears, right. But when someone else is using sign language, how do we listen? With our eyes! This next book will help us use our eyes to find the numbers in the pictures. Are you ready?

Book: *City by Numbers* by Stephen T. Johnson

Flannelboard activity/song: "How Many Candles on the Birthday Cake?" Make a simple cake shape and ten (or more) candles out of felt. Invite children up to put the candles on one by one and have the group count in sign language with each new addition. Then sing the following song (to the tune of "Happy Birthday"):

How many candles on the cake?

How many candles on the cake?

Can you help me count them?

How many candles on the cake?

One, two, three, four, five

Six, seven, eight, nine, ten.

Ten candles on our cake,

Ten candles on our cake.

Other materials to use with this theme:

Ten, Nine, Eight by Molly Bang
Clifford Counts Bubbles by Norman Bridwell
Benny's Pennies by Pat Brisson
1, 2, 3 to the Zoo: A Counting Book by Eric Carle
The Very Hungry Caterpillar by Eric Carle
One Red Rooster by Kathleen Sullivan Carroll
Ten Black Dots by Donald Crews
Two Ways to Count to Ten: A Liberian Folktale by Ruby Dee
Rosie's Roses by Pamela Duncan Edwards
Feast for Ten by Cathryn Falwell
Mama Cat Has Three Kittens by Denise Fleming
Sitting Down to Eat by Bill Harley
Splash! by Ann Jonas
Ten Apples up on Top! by Theo LeSeig
Ten Rosy Roses by Eve Merriam
Ten Red Apples by Virginia Miller
Toby Counts His Marbles by Cyndy Szekeres
Little Quack by Lauren Thompson
Dinnertime! by Sue Williams
"This Old Man" from *Kids' Favorite Songs 2*
"Five Little Monkeys" from *"So Big": Activity Songs for Little Ones* by Hap Palmer
"Ten in the Bed" from *The Elephant Show, Volume 1* by Sharon, Lois, and Bram

CHAPTER ELEVEN

Elementary School Programs

Catch the Olympic Spirit!

Program description: Celebrate the Olympic Games with facts, fun, and even some sign language.

Signs used in this program: RED, YELLOW, BLUE, BLACK, GREEN

Opening: Distribute flags (homemade or store bought) from different countries and have the participants march in the "Parade of Nations" using music from *Summon the Heroes* by John Williams and the Boston Pops Orchestra (New York: Sony Classical, 1996).

Opening ceremony: Have participants place flags around the room, then greet them formally and declare the official opening of the program. "Light" a paper torch to signal the opening of the program. Have the participants recite the Olympic oath, available at www.janecky.com/olympics/oath.html.

Book: *Olympics!* by B. G. Hennessy

Transition: The Olympic flag has five rings. Now let's learn what the rings represent. We'll learn the signs for the colors as we go.

Activity: Build the Olympic flag. Put each ring up on a white background as you discuss its meaning. (Find information about the Olympic logo at www.usolympicteam.com/19116_18922.htm.)

Jokes: Read a few riddles from *Olympic Jokes* by Jim Rothaus (Plymouth, Minn.: Child's World, 1997).

Games:

Who can stand on one foot the longest?

Long jump (mark the starting line with tape, then mark the spot where each participant lands with a sticker or piece of tape)

Cotton ball race (give each participant a cotton ball and have them race by blowing the cotton balls lengthwise along a table)

Craft: Make Olympic medals using gold posterboard and ribbon.

Closing ceremony: Award the medals and play fanfare.
Other materials to use with this theme:
 Elympics by X. J. Kennedy

Play with Your Food

Program description: Most of the time, it's not polite to play with your food
 . . . but in our silly hands-on storytime, that's exactly what we're going to
 do! Join us for wacky stories, songs, sign language, and edible crafts that
 will have you smacking your lips and asking for more!
Signs used in this program: EAT/FOOD, PLAY, STICKY, CHEWING-
 GUM
Opening song: "If You're Hungry and You Know It"
 If you're hungry and you know it, rub your tummy. . . .
 If you're hungry and you know it, pick up your fork. . . .
 If you're hungry and you know it, chow down. . . .
Book: *How Are You Peeling? Foods with Moods* by Saxton Freymann
Poem: "Never Take a Pig to Lunch" from *Never Take a Pig to Lunch and Other
 Poems about the Fun of Eating,* selected by Nadine Bernard Westcott (New
 York: Orchard Books, 1994).
Song: "Bubblegum" from *The Baby Record* by Bob McGrath and Katharine
 Smithram (Use the signs STICKY and CHEWING-GUM as you sing this
 song.)
Book: *Sam's Sandwich* by David Pelham (New York: Dutton, 1991)
Rhyme: "Who Stole the Cookies from the Cookie Jar?" (traditional)
 (Have everyone sit in a circle and clap their hands or tap out a rhythm on
 their laps as you recite the rhyme. Go around the circle and use each
 child's name in turn.)
 Who stole the cookies from the cookie jar?
 Who, me? Yes, you!
 Can't be! Then who?
 ———— stole the cookies from the cookie jar!
 Who, me? Yes, you!
 Can't be! Then who?
 (Repeat until all children's names have been used. For a funny ending, use
 your name last, and when you say "Can't be!" pull real or fake cookies out
 of your pockets.)
Flannelboard story: Ice Cream Scoops
 (Make a cone and several different colored scoops of ice cream from felt.)
 Once upon a time there was a little boy named Tommy. Tommy LOVED

ice cream. One day he decided to go to the corner ice cream shop. But when he got there, he couldn't decide what flavor to get.

"Should I get vanilla?" he asked. He decided to get one scoop of vanilla on his ice cream cone.

But then he saw the chocolate. He decided to get a scoop of that too.

(Repeat with strawberry, fudge ripple, pistachio, bubblegum, and so on until the ice cream cone is towering high on the flannelboard.)

Finally he was ready to eat his ice cream come. Slurp! He ate the (begin with last scoop and repeat until all the flavors are eaten). Then he ate the cone with a crunch crunch crunch.

"Oh no! Now I have a tummyache!" said Tommy.

Book: Show pictures from *Play with Your Food* by Joost Elffers (New York: Stewart, Tabori, and Chang, 1997).

Food craft ideas:

Celery puppets: Provide each child with a piece of celery and cream cheese or peanut butter for filling. Then use raisins, nuts, or dried fruit to make faces on the "puppets."

Celery and carrot cars: Use a piece of celery as the body of the car, and provide circular pieces of carrot for wheels. Attach the wheels using toothpicks, and decorate with raisins, nuts, and dried fruit (using cream cheese or peanut butter as adhesive).

Rice-cake sea scenes: Use blue food coloring to dye regular cream cheese. Spread this on the rice cake to represent the sea. Use goldfish crackers, pieces of lettuce, and dried fruit to create an underwater scene.

Tootsie Roll sculptures: Rub the candy between your fingers to make it warm and pliant, then mold it into whatever shape you like (some ideas: a teddy bear, a dragon, a dinosaur, an alligator).

Other materials to use with this theme:

Today Is Monday by Eric Carle

Sitting Down to Eat by Bill Harley

If You Give a Mouse a Cookie by Laura Numeroff

"Silly Pizza Song" from *Signing Time Songs, Volumes 1–3* by Rachel de Azevedo Coleman

"Going on a Picnic" from *The Corner Grocery Store* by Raffi

"Popcorn" from *The Corner Grocery Store* by Raffi

My Mother Ate . . . game (see appendix C)

Pass the Food game (see appendix C)

Sign Language School

Program description: Learn basic school signs through stories, songs, and more, focusing on American Sign Language.

Signs used in this program: HELLO, SCHOOL, MOUSE, BALL, BOOK, WRITE, NO, PAY-ATTENTION

Introduction: (Begin by going to the front of the room and silently signing HELLO until everyone repeats the sign.) Do you know what I just said? Hello! But I said it in American Sign Language! Today we're going to be learning about American Sign Language, which is a language that uses our hands and eyes instead of our mouths and ears. Do you know who uses sign language? Many deaf people use it to communicate every day, but you don't have to be deaf to learn it. In this first story, you'll meet a little boy who is deaf and see what his school is like. Think about how his school is like yours and different from yours as we read the story.

Book: *Moses Goes to School* by Isaac Millman** (Teach signs in the story as you read, but skip the song for now.)

Discussion: Is Moses's school like your school? How is it the same and how is it different? How are hearing and deaf people alike?

Song: Teach "Take Me Out to the Ballgame" using the signs in *Moses Goes to School*. Teach it line by line, and then have the participants sing and sign once you are ready to put the whole thing together.

Transition: Now let's give your hands a little rest. I'm going to show you a book that encourages us to use something else that's important in sign language—our eyes.

Book: *Mouse Views: What the Class Pet Saw* by Bruce McMillan

Discussion: Sometimes we have to learn to see things in a different way. If you want to understand American Sign Language, you need to learn to use your eyes to see small things. Our hands and eyes are very important in sign language, but so are our faces. I'm going to sign the sign NO in two different ways but do different things with my face. Can you tell the difference? (Sign NO once in an "oh, go on, it can't be" sort of way and once in a "for the thousandth time, I said *no*" sort of way)

Game: "Face Your Feelings" from *Learn to Sign the Fun Way* by Penny Warner**

Book: *Froggy Goes to School* by Jonathan London

Song: "Wiggle in My Toe" from *Late Last Night* by Joe Scruggs

Other materials to use with this theme:

   Today Is Monday by Eric Carle

   A Fine, Fine School by Sharon Creech

   Two Ways to Count to Ten: A Liberian Folktale by Ruby Dee

   The Seals on the Bus by Lenny Hort

   Moses Goes to a Concert by Isaac Millman**

   If You Take a Mouse to School by Laura Numeroff

Minerva Louise at School by Janet Morgan Stoeke

"I Went to School One Morning" from *Sing a Song of Seasons* by Rachel Buchman

Name Plaques craft (see appendix C)

Same and Different game (see appendix C)

Sign Language Fun

Program description: Flex your fingers and open your eyes wide—it's time to learn some American Sign Language! Learn about the fascinating history of ASL, and join in with some simple signs.

Signs used in this program: HELLO, SIGN, LANGUAGE, DEAF, HEARING-PERSON, DOG, SCHOOL, NO, YES, AMERICA, READ, WRITE, letters A–Z

Opening: (Teach sign for HELLO.) Today we're going to learn about sign language. Here's how you sign SIGN LANGUAGE. (Demonstrate signs.) Who knows what sign language is? It's a language that uses our eyes and hands and faces rather than our mouths and voices. Who uses sign language? Deaf people. Here's the sign for DEAF. (Demonstrate sign.) What does *deaf* mean? Someone who can't hear, right? But do only deaf people use sign language? Can HEARING (teach sign) people learn it too? Sure they can! Why do you think this is the sign for HEARING-PERSON? Because that's what it looks like when we talk. Everything in sign language is meant for your eyes, not your ears.

Book: *Buffy's Orange Leash* by Stephen Golder and Lise Memling**

Activity: The Story of ASL (see appendix C)

Book: *The Handmade Alphabet* by Laura Rankin**

Discussion: When do we use the manual alphabet, or fingerspelling? (for names, brand names, and so on) Can you imagine trying to fingerspell every single letter if you wanted to say something? It would take you all day! (Have the kids try to spell out a whole sentence to demonstrate.)

Craft: Name Plaques craft (see appendix C)

Other materials to use with this theme:

Secret Signs: Along the Underground Railroad by Anita Riggio**

The Printer by Myron Uhlberg**

The Alphabet Game (see appendix C)

I-L-Y Flowers craft (see appendix C)

I-L-Y Stick Puppets craft (see appendix C)

TTY game (see appendix C)

CHAPTER TWELVE

Middle School Programs

What's Your Sign (Language)?

Program description: Learn the very basics about American Sign Language through games and other fun activities. Warm up your hands and prepare to join in as we learn signs and explore Deaf Culture and history.

Signs used in this program: TRUE, FALSE, SIGN, LANGUAGE, DEAF, HEARING-PERSON, SCHOOL, NO, YES, AMERICA, READ, WRITE

Introduction: Go around the room and have the participants introduce themselves and what they hope to learn.

Activity: Deaf Culture True and False (see appendix C)

Game: Silent Birthday Line-Up (see appendix C)

Discussion: The importance of facial expression in ASL

Game: "Face Your Feelings" from *Learn to Sign the Fun Way* by Penny Warner**

Activity: The Story of ASL (see appendix C)

Game: "SIGNO" from *Learn to Sign the Fun Way* by Penny Warner**

Other materials to use with this program:
Handtalk Birthday by Remy Charlip, Mary Beth, and George Ancona**
Secret Signs: Along the Underground Railroad by Anita Riggio**
The Printer by Myron Uhlberg**
Charades (see appendix C)
Drawing Shapes game (see appendix C)

Talk with Your Hands, Listen with Your Eyes

Program description: Explore American Sign Language through games and interactive activities. This session focuses on the manual alphabet, simple signs, and using our eyes.

Signs used in this program: DEAF, AMERICA, SIGN, LANGUAGE, letters A–Z, HELLO, SAME, DIFFERENT

Introduction: Welcome to our program! Today we're going to talk about American Sign Language. I'm sure most of you know that American Sign Language is used by many deaf people. Here's the sign for DEAF. (Demonstrate sign.) Let me ask you a question: Do deaf people all over the world use American Sign Language? (Teach signs AMERICA, SIGN, LANGUAGE.) No. There are many different sign languages all over the world, just as there are many different spoken languages. American Sign Language is used in the United States and Canada. When using a sign language, you don't use only your hands; you also have to use your eyes to listen. That can sometimes be hard to get used to for people who are used to using their ears. Today we're going to play some games that will teach us how to use our eyes to understand signs.

Game: Who's the Leader? (see appendix C)

Discussion: Was the game easy or difficult? Was it hard to concentrate on just using your eyes and not your voice?

Game: Drawing Shapes (see appendix C)

Activity: Introduce the manual alphabet using a transparency or handout of the letters. Go through the letters with the group at least twice. The first time, go slowly and check to make sure that everyone is making the letters properly. The second time, go through the letters more quickly. Then invite the group to spell a few simple words together, such as cat, mop, dog, and owl. End this section by asking each person to spell his or her name.

Game: Same and Different (see appendix C)

Game: Fingerspelling Circle (see appendix C)

Game: Go Fish with Names (see appendix C)

Other materials to use with this program:

The Turn-Around, Upside-Down Alphabet Book by Lisa Campbell Ernst

Alphabet City by Stephen T. Johnson

Mouse Views: What the Class Pet Saw by Bruce McMillan

The City ABC Book by Zoran Milich

The Handmade Alphabet by Laura Rankin**

The Alphabet Game (see appendix C)

Handshape Pins craft (see appendix C)

Name Plaques craft (see appendix C)

TTY game (see appendix C)

Animal Signs

Program description: Learn basic American Sign Language through games and hands-on activities exploring the world of animals.

Signs used in this program: DEAF, HEARING-PERSON, AMERICA, SIGN, LANGUAGE, MOOSE, MOUSE, other animal signs of your choice

Introduction: Today we're going to be discussing American Sign Language. (Teach signs AMERICA, SIGN, LANGUAGE.) American Sign Language, or ASL, is used by many people who are DEAF (teach sign) here in the United States and also in Canada. There are many different sign languages all over the world. HEARING (teach sign) people can also learn sign language, and it's a lot of fun! The most important thing is learning to use your eyes and your hands instead of your ears and your mouth. Today we're going to play some games that teach animal signs. Some of the games will be voices-off, which means we use only our hands and eyes to communicate.

Icebreaker game: Charades: Animals (see appendix C)

Game: Moose (see appendix C)

Eyes and ears at the zoo: Show a picture book or video about a trip to the zoo. Invite participants to identify first all the sounds represented. Then ask them to "turn off their ears" and focus on what they can experience through their eyes. Discuss the results. Are the things we can tell with our ears better than, equal to, or worse than what our eyes tell us?

Assistive devices: Using a catalog from Harris Communications or another company that specializes in assistive devices for the deaf, introduce the concepts of flashing doorbells, flashing or vibrating alarm clocks, and TTYs. Emphasize that each of these devices provides an equal experience for deaf people but focuses on the visual sense rather than on sound.

Game: I Went to the Zoo (see appendix C)

Game: Repeat the game Moose if time allows.

Other materials to use with this program:

Handtalk Zoo by George Ancona and Mary Beth**

Two Ways to Count to Ten: A Liberian Folktale by Ruby Dee

Buffy's Orange Leash by Stephen Golder and Lise Memling**

"Supermachine: A Play" from Let's Learn about Deafness: Classroom Activities by Rachel Stone-Harris**

TTY game (see appendix C)

A Feast of Sign Language

Program description: Learn basic sign language through hands-on activities and games about food and colors.

Signs used in this program: EAT/FOOD, AMERICA, SIGN, LANGUAGE, PIZZA, RED, YELLOW, GREEN, ORANGE, BLUE, PURPLE, PINK, BLACK, RAINBOW, MY, MOTHER, food signs of your choice

Introduction: Everybody eats, right? (Teach the sign for EAT/FOOD.) Today we're going to learn some basic American Sign Language (teach signs AMERICA, SIGN, LANGUAGE) by focusing on food. We'll not only learn food and color signs but also practice using our eyes and ears in different ways. American Sign Language is a visual language, which means it's very different from spoken language. Spoken languages use sounds, but visual languages use gestures. This means that, to become good at a visual language, you need to learn not only the language but also new ways of using your hands and eyes—and your whole body! You might feel a bit silly doing some of the activities at first, but they will all help you to learn ASL more easily.

Game: Mirror Game (see appendix C)

Game: Pass the Food (see appendix C)

Song: "Silly Pizza Song" from *Signing Time Songs, Volumes 1–3* by Rachel de Azevedo Coleman. (To incorporate even more food signs into this song for older kids, make a pizza base and large laminated pictures of ten to fifteen different foods and tape them to a wall as you stack them up. To speed up the song, add two or three items with each verse. Sing the song together without the music instead of sticking to the foods on the album. This is a very popular activity with middle schoolers, especially if you add silly things such as water, hot dogs, and ice cream to your pizza.)

Activity: Teach color signs.

Game: Drawing Shapes: Color Variation (see appendix C)

Game: Colorful Squares *or* Pass the Colors (see appendix C)

Game: My Mother Ate . . . (see appendix C). Encourage kids to combine colors and foods in their answers for this game (e.g., "My mother ate one red apple. . . .").

Other materials to use with this program:

Handtalk Zoo by George Ancona and Mary Beth**

"Crazy Categories" from *Learn to Sign the Fun Way* by Penny Warner**

All My Neighbors game (see appendix C)

Charades: Food (see appendix C)

TTY game (see appendix C)

CHAPTER THIRTEEN

Family Programs

Fall Frolic

Program description: Fall into our fun autumnal storytime, featuring stories, songs, and even signs for the whole family!

Signs used in this program: FALL, PUMPKIN, APPLE, numbers 1–5

Opening song: "If You're Happy and You Know It" from *Kids' Favorite Songs 2*

Book: *I Know It's Autumn* by Eileen Spinelli or *Clifford's First Autumn* by Norman Bridwell

Song: "Five Little Leaves" from *Sing a Song of Seasons* by Rachel Buchman

Book: *Fall Leaves Fall* by Zoe Hall

Flannelboard rhyme: "Five Little Pumpkins"
(Teach PUMPKIN and numbers 1–5 to use with this rhyme.)
Five little pumpkins, sitting by my door;
I gave one to my mother, and now there are four.
Four little pumpkins, such a sight to see;
I gave one to my father, and now there are three.
Three little pumpkins, I knew what to do;
I gave one to my sister, and now there are two.
Two little pumpkins, sitting in the sun;
I gave one to my brother, and now there is one.
One little pumpkin, isn't this fun?
I gave one to you, and now there are none.

Book: *Five Little Pumpkins* by Iris Van Rynbach or *Plumply, Dumply Pumpkin* by Mary Serfozo

Rhyme: "Up in the Apple Tree" (Use signs for APPLE and numbers 1–3.)
Way up high in the apple tree

The apples said, "You can't get me!"
And I shook and I shook and I shook that tree,
And down fell the apples one, two, three!
Crunch!

Song: "Get Up and Go" from *We All Live Together, Volume 5* by Greg and Steve

Other materials to use with this theme:

A Fine, Fine School by Sharon Creech
It's Fall! by Linda Glaser
The Apple Pie Tree by Zoe Hall
It's Pumpkin Time! by Zoe Hall
What Can You Do in the Wind? by Anna Grossnickle Hines
The Seals on the Bus by Lenny Hort
Ten Apples up on Top! by Theo LeSeig
Froggy Goes to School by Jonathan London
Ten Red Apples by Virginia Miller
If You Take a Mouse to School by Laura Numeroff
Apples and Pumpkins by Anne Rockwell
Fall Is for Friends by Suzy Spafford
I Know It's Autumn by Eileen Spinelli
Apples, Apples, Apples by Nancy Elizabeth Wallace
Apple Farmer Annie by Monica Wellington
"Five Little Leaves" from *Sing a Song of Seasons* by Rachel Buchman
"I Like the Fall" from *Sing a Song of Seasons* by Rachel Buchman
"Over the River and through the Woods" from *Children's Favorite Songs 3* by Larry Groce and the Disneyland Children's Sing-Along Chorus
"Five Little Pumpkins" from *Singable Songs for the Very Young* by Raffi
"Five Green Apples" from *Mainly Mother Goose* by Sharon, Lois, and Bram

Wonderful Wintertime!

Program description: The snow is falling, the air is cold, and it's time to cuddle up with wonderful stories of wintertime. Join us for stories, songs, rhymes, and even some sign language for the whole family.

Signs used in this program: WINTER, SNOW, numbers 1–5

Opening song: "Snow Song" from *Hello Everybody! Playsongs and Rhymes from a Toddler's World* by Rachel Buchman

Teach signs: WINTER, SNOW

Book: *Snip, Snip . . . Snow!* by Nancy Poydar or *Good Night, Baby Bear* by Frank Asch

Flannelboard rhyme: "Five Little Snowflakes"
(Teach numbers 1–5 to use with this rhyme.)
The air was cold in the town,
and one little snowflake started drifting down.
The air grew colder in the town;
Now two little snowflakes are drifting down.
The wind started blowing in the town;
Now three little snowflakes are drifting down.
The air grew frosty in the town;
Now four little snowflakes are drifting down.
It's colder than ever in the town,
And five little snowflakes are drifting down.

Book: *Kipper's Snowy Day* by Mick Inkpen or *Cleo in the Snow* by Caroline Mockford

Song: "Rock and Roll Freeze Dance" from *"So Big": Activity Songs for Little Ones* by Hap Palmer

Book: *Snow on Snow on Snow* by Cheryl Chapman or *Bunny's First Snowflake* by Monica Wellington

Rhyme: "Snowman"
I built a snowman, round and fat.
I gave him eyes, nose, and a hat,
A mouth to smile, a scarf of felt,
But the sun came out, and he started to melt!

Song: "Jingle Bells" from *Christmas Magic* by Joanie Bartels (Pass out jingle bells and have everyone play and sing along.)

Other materials to use with this theme:
Snowballs by Lois Ehlert
David's Drawings by Cathryn Falwell
A Winter Day by Douglas Florian
What Can You Do in the Snow? by Anna Grossnickle Hines
The Snowy Day by Ezra Jack Keats
The First Snowfall by Anne and Harlow Rockwell
Where Did Bunny Go? by Nancy Tafuri
"Mitten Weather" from *Sing a Song of Seasons* by Rachel Buchman
"Let's Play in the Snow" from *Sing a Song of Seasons* by Rachel Buchman

Spring Is Here!

Program description: Welcome the warmer weather with stories, songs, and signs for all ages about spring.

Signs used in this program: SPRING, CATERPILLAR, BUTTERFLY, FLOWER, numbers 1–5

Opening song: "You Are My Sunshine" (traditional)

Book: *Wake Up, It's Spring!* by Lisa Campbell Ernst or *It's Spring!* by Else Holmelund Minarik

Rhyme: "In the Spring"

In the spring the sun does shine,
The birds fly to and fro.
The frogs say "Ribbit" in the pond,
And the flowers grow!

Book: *Farfellina and Marcel* by Holly Keller or *The Very Hungry Caterpillar* by Eric Carle (Teach the signs CATERPILLAR and BUTTERFLY in these stories.)

Action rhyme: "Caterpillar, Caterpillar"

(Use the signs CATERPILLAR and BUTTERFLY with this rhyme.)
Caterpillar, caterpillar, turn around.
Caterpillar, caterpillar, on the ground.
Caterpillar, caterpillar, climb up high.
Soon you'll be a butterfly!

Book: *Muncha! Muncha! Muncha!* by Candace Fleming

Flannelboard: "Five Little Flowers"

(Teach FLOWER and numbers 1–5 to use during this rhyme.)
Five little flowers grew by my door;
I picked one for my mother, and then there were four.
Four little flowers pretty as can be;
I picked one for my father, and then there were three.
Three little flowers, what could I do?
I picked one for my sister, and then there were two.
Two little flowers out in the sun;
I picked one for my brother, and then there was one.
One little flower, isn't this fun?
I picked one for you, and then there were none.

Book: *Fran's Flower* by Lisa Bruce or *Rosie's Roses* by Pamela Duncan Edwards

Song: "The Bunny Hop" from *Disney's Dance Along, Volume 1*

Other materials to use with this theme:

Rabbits and Raindrops by Jim Arnosky
Duckie's Rainbow by Frances Barry
Rabbit's Good News by Ruth Lercher Bornstein
In the Spring by Craig Brown

Flora's Surprise by Debi Gliori
In the Rain with Baby Duck by Amy Hest
Spot Goes to the Farm by Eric Hill
What Can You Do in the Rain? by Anna Grossnickle Hines
Kipper's Rainy Day by Mick Inkpen
Yellow Umbrella by Jae Soo Liu
Ten Rosy Roses by Eve Merriam
I Kissed the Baby! by Mary Murphy
I Spy in the Garden by Richard Powell
Growing Like Me by Anne Rockwell
My Spring Robin by Anne Rockwell
Two Blue Jays by Anne Rockwell
Rainy Day by Janet Morgan Stoeke
Bear Wants More by Karma Wilson
"When the Pod Went Pop!" from *Sing a Song of Seasons* by Rachel Buchman

Super Summertime

Program description: If the sun is shining and the days are hotter, it must be time for our summer storytime full of stories, songs, and signs for the whole family!

Signs used in this program: SUMMER, numbers 1–5, BLUE, RED, YELLOW, GREEN, PURPLE

Opening song: "A Walking We Will Go" from *We All Live Together, Volume 5* by Greg and Steve

Book: *D. W. All Wet* by Marc Brown or *Splash!* by Flora McDonnell

Song: "Swimmy Swim" from *Sing a Song of Seasons* by Rachel Buchman

Prop story: "The Bath" from *Henry and Mudge in the Green Time* by Cynthia Rylant

Song: "The Swim" from *Disney's Dance Along, Volume 1*

Flannelboard rhyme: "Five Beach Umbrellas" (Use color and number signs.)
I went to the beach and sat under the sun;
I put up my blue umbrella, and that was number one.
My sister came along; she brought an umbrella too.
She set up her red umbrella, and that was number two.
My brother came next; he called and waved to me.
And he set up a yellow umbrella, and that was number three.
My mother finally got there; now we only need one more.
She set up a green umbrella, and that was number four.

At last my father came, the last one to arrive.

He set up a purple umbrella, and that was number five.

Book: *Sea, Sand, Me!* by Patricia Hubbell or *A Beach Day* by Douglas Florian

Activity: Surfing

Spread beach towels out on the floor and pretend they are surfboards. Play surfing music (such as *Muppet Beach Party*, New York: Jim Henson Records, 1993) in the background, and invite the kids to pretend surf. Direct them in several specific activities, such as paddling, riding a big wave, and wiping out.

Closing song: "Round and Round We Go" from *It's Toddler Time* by Carol Hammett and Elaine Bueffel

Other materials to use with this theme:

Maisy Goes Swimming by Lucy Cousins

One Hot Summer Day by Nina Crews

A Summer Day by Douglas Florian

Spot Visits His Grandparents by Eric Hill

What Can You Do in the Sun? by Anna Grossnickle Hines

Kipper's Sunny Day by Mick Inkpen

Splash! by Ann Jonas

How Will We Get to the Beach? A Guessing-Game Story by Brigitte Luciani

Splish, Splash by Jeff Sheppard

Mouse's First Summer by Lauren Thompson

"Here Is a Beehive" from *Sing a Song of Seasons* by Rachel Buchman

"Going on a Picnic" from *The Corner Grocery Store* by Raffi

"Mr. Sun" from *Singable Songs for the Very Young* by Raffi

"Ants in My Pants" from *Late Last Night* by Joe Scruggs

Sign Language at the Zoo

Program description: Pat your paws, flail your flippers, and warm up your fingers—it's time to learn animal signs through stories and songs!

Signs used in this program: Z-O-O (spelled), ELEPHANT, LION, SNAKE, MONKEY, NO (NONE), PLAY, BIRD, TIGER, BEAR, SEAL, HIPPO-POTAMUS, numbers 1–10

Song: "Going to the Zoo" from *Singable Songs for the Very Young* by Raffi

Introduction: Today we're going to learn American Sign Language signs for different animals at the zoo! Maybe you know the sounds that different animals make. Who knows what sound an elephant makes? . . . That's right. Well, when we do sign language, we don't make any sounds—we use our hands to make the signs and our eyes to see them. Many deaf people, or people who can't hear, use American Sign Language. But you can learn signs whether you are deaf or not! This first story has lots of animals in it. Let's learn the signs, and then later we'll see how many you remember.

Book: *Dear Zoo* by Rod Campbell

Activity rhyme: "Five Little Monkeys" (traditional)
(Teach NO [NONE] and numbers 1–5 to use with this rhyme.)
Five little monkeys jumping on the bed; one fell off and bumped his head. Mama called the doctor and the doctor said, "No more monkeys jumping on the bed!"
Four little monkeys . . .
Three little monkeys . . .
Two little monkeys . . .
One little monkey . . .
No little monkeys . . .

Flannelboard rhyme: "Zoo Noises" (Use this to reinforce signs learned earlier.)
I went to the zoo, and what did I hear?
I heard a _____ and it said _____.

Book: *Playtime for Zoo Animals* by Caroline Arnold

Song: "One Elephant Went Out to Play" from *The Elephant Show, Volume 1* by Sharon, Lois, and Bram

Book: *1, 2, 3 to the Zoo!* by Eric Carle (Teach or reinforce the signs for the animals as you tell the story.)

Activity: Zoo Train
Make simple masks of different animals, and invite each child to put one on and join the zoo train. Review the sign for each animal as you distribute the masks. Play marching music and lead the children around the room or through the library.

Other materials to use with this theme:
We're Going on a Lion Hunt by David Axtell
How Many Kisses Do You Want Tonight? by Varsha Bajaj
Whose Nose and Toes? by John Butler
Do You Want to Be My Friend? by Eric Carle
From Head to Toe by Eric Carle
Today Is Monday by Eric Carle
Two Ways to Count to Ten: A Liberian Folktale by Ruby Dee
Sitting Down to Eat by Bill Harley
The Seals on the Bus by Lenny Hort
Splash! by Ann Jonas

My *Camera at the Zoo* by Janet Perry Marshall
Splash! by Flora McDonnell
Toddlerobics: Animal Fun by Zita Newcome
Sam Who Never Forgets by Eve Rice
Dinnertime! by Sue Williams
"Three Little Monkeys" from *It's Toddler Time* by Carol Hammett and
    Elaine Bueffel
"Five Little Monkeys" from *"So Big": Activity Songs for Little Ones* by Hap
    Palmer
"Willoughby Wallaby Woo" from *Singable Songs for the Very Young* by Raffi

Sign Language Is Yummy!

Program description: Join us for a feast of food signs! We'll learn together through stories, music, and activities for the whole family.

Signs used in this program: EAT/FOOD, SIGN, LANGUAGE, APPLE, PIZZA, CRACKER, ICE-CREAM, CEREAL, BREAD, COOKIE, BANANA, CANDY, CHEESE, MILK, EGG, HONEY, THANK-YOU

Introduction: Today we are going to learn about American Sign Language. Do you know what sign language is? It is a language that uses our hands and eyes instead of our mouths and ears. Deaf people use sign language. What does *deaf* mean? It means someone who can't hear. Let me ask you a question: Do *only* deaf people use sign language? No! Hearing people can learn it too. Here's how we say SIGN LANGUAGE (teach signs SIGN, LANGUAGE) in sign language! Today we are going to learn signs about one of my favorite things—FOOD! (Teach sign EAT/FOOD.)

Flannelboard story: "Goldilocks and the Three Bears" (Tell this story using signs from *Beyond Words: Great Stories for Hands and Voice* by Valerie Marsh**)

Fingerplay: (Sign the words in capital letters.)
    When I'm hungry, I like to EAT
    An APPLE, a CRACKER, or something sweet!

Song: "Silly Pizza Song" from *Signing Time Songs, Volumes 1–3* by Rachel de Azevedo Coleman

Book: *Baby's Breakfast* by Emilie Poulsson

Song: "Shake My Sillies Out" from *More Singable Songs* by Raffi

Other materials to use with this theme:
    Today Is Monday by Eric Carle
    The Very Hungry Caterpillar by Eric Carle
    Feast for Ten by Cathryn Falwell

Sitting Down to Eat by Bill Harley
Spot Bakes a Cake by Eric Hill
If You Give a Mouse a Cookie by Laura Numeroff
It's My Birthday by Helen Oxenbury
Tickle Tum! by Nancy Van Laan
Bunny Cakes by Rosemary Wells
Dinnertime! by Sue Williams
Bear Wants More by Karma Wilson
"When the Pod Went Pop!" from *Sing a Song of Seasons* by Rachel Buchman
"Cluck, Cluck, Red Hen" from *The Corner Grocery Store* by Raffi
"Going on a Picnic" from *The Corner Grocery Store* by Raffi
"Popcorn" from *The Corner Grocery Store* by Raffi
"Ants in My Pants" from *Late Last Night* by Joe Scruggs
"On a Picnic We Will Go" from *The Elephant Show, Volume 1* by Sharon, Lois, and Bram
Charades: Food (see appendix C)
My Mother Ate . . . game (see appendix C)
Pass the Food game (see appendix C)

My Sign Language A-B-C

Program description: Explore the alphabet in a whole new way as we learn some sign language through stories, songs, and fun activities! Join us for the ABCs and much more!

Signs used in this program: Letters A–Z, SIGN

Opening song: "Letters Everywhere" (to the tune of "The Farmer in the Dell")

(Encourage children to write their names in the air as if writing on a blackboard.)

There are letters everywhere, there are letters everywhere.
You have letters in your name, there are letters everywhere.
Can you write your name? Can you write your name?
Move your finger in the air to write write write your name.

Introduction: Wow, that was a great workout! We really warmed up our hands by writing in the air like that. But there's another way to say our names with our hands—we could use American Sign Language! That's what we're going to talk about today. American Sign Language is a different language from English. We don't speak it with our mouths and listen to it with our ears—we sign it with our hands and listen to it with our eyes! Today we're going to learn the signs for the letters of the alphabet. This first book will teach us the letters, and then we will practice them throughout our program.

Book: *The Handmade Alphabet* by Laura Rankin**

Song: "The Alphabet Song" (traditional)

A B C D E F G,

H I J K L M N O P,

Q R S,

T U V,

W X,

Y and Z.

Now we've sung our ABCs;

Next time won't you SIGN with me?

Book or flannelboard story: *Chicka Chicka Boom Boom* by Bill Martin Jr.

Song: "Bingo" from *Great Big Hits 2* by Sharon, Lois, and Bram

Flannelboard game: "I Spy Something That Starts With . . ."

Make flannelboard pieces showing various objects that start with different letters, such as flowers, apples, balls, elephants, and so on. (The easiest way to assemble this activity is to take single pieces from other flannelboards.) Put four objects that start with different letters on the flannelboard, and recite the rhyme below:

I see four things, four things I see.

Can you say what they are with me?

A _____, a _____, a _____, and a _____.

But which is the one that starts with (sign letter)?

Use this activity to reinforce letter signs and sounds. For an additional signing activity, choose only objects that you know the signs for, and teach those signs as well. This activity could also be done using small objects such as stuffed animals and office supplies, or with volunteers whose names start with different letters.

Book: *ABC Kids* by Laura Ellen Williams

Song: "The Name Game" from *Great Big Hits 2* by Sharon, Lois, and Bram

Transition: Remember, we don't use only our hands in American Sign Language. It's also very important to use our eyes to see the signs. This book will help us practice seeing things in different ways.

Book: *The Turn-Around, Upside-Down Alphabet Book* by Lisa Campbell Ernst

Song: "Alphabet Song" (traditional)

A B C D E F G,

H I J K L M N O P,

Q R S,

T U V,
W X,
Y and Z.
Now we've SIGNED our ABCs;
Show your favorite letter to me!
Other materials to use with this theme:
Q Is for Duck: An Alphabet Guessing Game by Mary Elting and Michael
 Folsom
The Letters Are Lost by Lisa Campbell Ernst
ABC for You and Me by Meg Girnis
Kipper's A to Z: An Alphabet Adventure by Mick Inkpen
Alphabet City by Stephen T. Johnson
The City ABC Book by Zoran Milich
"The Bajan Alphabet Song" from Jump Up and Sing: Binyah's Favorite
 Songs
The Alphabet Game (see appendix C)
Handshape Pins craft (see appendix C)
Name Plaques game (see appendix C)

Let's Sign Together

Program description: Bring the whole family for a fun exploration of American Sign Language through stories, songs, and hands-on activities.

Signs used in this program: SIGN, TOGETHER, RABBIT, FATHER, MOTHER, EAT/FOOD, PLAY, BOOK, PLEASE, SHARE, TURN, THANK-YOU

Introduction: Today we're going to learn to SIGN. (Demonstrate sign.) That means sign. Can you do the sign with me? We're going to learn some American Sign Language. Some people think that sign language is only for people who are deaf, which means they can't hear. But sign language is for everyone! And it's the most fun when we all sign together! Here's the sign for TOGETHER. (Demonstrate sign.) Let's sign it during this next song.

Opening song: "We're All Together Again" from We All Live Together, Volume 5 by Greg and Steve

Book: Bunny Day: Telling Time from Breakfast to Bedtime by Rick Walton

Song: "Magic Words" from Signing Time Songs, Volumes 1–3 by Rachel de Azevedo Coleman

Book: Moses Goes to the Circus by Isaac Millman**

Song: "As I Was Walking to Town One Day" from The Baby Record by Bob

McGrath and Katharine Smithram (Use this song to teach additional animal signs, or adapt it to reinforce the animal signs in the story.)

Book: *Just Like Daddy* by Frank Asch or *Mama Cat Has Three Kittens* by Denise Fleming

Song: "The More We Get Together" from *Singable Songs for the Very Young* by Raffi

Other materials to use with this theme:

Good Night, Baby Bear by Frank Asch

How Many Kisses Do You Want Tonight? by Varsha Bajaj

Benny's Pennies by Pat Brisson

The Biggest Bed in the World by Lindsay Camp

Snowballs by Lois Ehlert

Wake Up, It's Spring! by Lisa Campbell Ernst

Feast for Ten by Cathryn Falwell

Nicky and Grandpa by Cathryn Falwell

Time for Bed by Mem Fox

Sitting Down to Eat by Bill Harley

Spot Bakes a Cake by Eric Hill

Spot Visits His Grandparents by Eric Hill

Dad and Me in the Morning by Patricia Lakin**

Baby Loves Hugs and Kisses by Michael Lawrence

Family by Helen Oxenbury

Come Along, Daisy! by Jane Simmons

Little Quack by Lauren Thompson

The Printer by Myron Uhlberg**

Tickle Tum! by Nancy Van Laan

Bunny Cakes by Rosemary Wells

"Proud to Be Me" from *Signing Time Songs, Volumes 1–3* by Rachel de Azevedo Coleman

"The Family" from *Wee Sing for Baby* by Pamela Conn Beall and Susan Hagen Nipp

"The Farmer in the Dell" from *Old MacDonald Had a Farm* by the Countdown Kids

"Here We Go Round the Mulberry Bush" from *Old MacDonald Had a Farm* by the Countdown Kids

"The Sharing Song" from *Singable Songs for the Very Young* by Raffi

"Ten in the Bed" from *The Elephant Show, Volume 1* by Sharon, Lois, and Bram

I-L-Y Stick Puppets craft (see appendix C)

APPENDIX A

Annotated Bibliography
of ASL Resources

Resources to Help You Learn ASL

American Sign Language Clip and Create 2. Wheaton, MD: Institute for Disabilities Research and Training, Inc., 2003–2004.

> More than just clip-art software, this CD includes graphics of more than three thousand signs, each accompanied by an English gloss and a pictorial representation of the concept. (See appendix E for samples.) This is a great way to learn signs for storytimes or to create materials from crossword puzzles to posters using the versatile printing features of the software.

Baby See 'n Sign Volume 1. Creswell, OR: Kronz Kids Productions, 2001.

Baby See 'n Sign Volume 2. Creswell, OR: Kronz Kids Productions, 2003.

> Johanna Larsen-Muhr, a CODA (child of deaf adults) and native signer, hosts these videos. A variety of youngsters demonstrate the signs, which are well chosen for young children and are repeated several times.

Bahan, Ben, and Joe Dannis. *Signs for Me: Basic Sign Vocabulary for Children, Parents, and Teachers*. San Diego: DawnSignPress, 1990.

> This classic ASL resource features an in-depth introduction, easy-to-follow line drawings, and illustrations for each concept presented.

Chambers, Diane. *Communicating in Sign: Creative Ways to Learn American Sign Language*. New York: Fireside, 1998.

> This more in-depth look at American Sign Language delves into grammar and structure as well as basic vocabulary.

Flodin, Mickey. *Signing for Kids*. New York: Putnam, 1991.

> This manual presents an enormous number of signs in an easy-to-follow, large format. Topics include the manual alphabet, pets and animals, food, sports, school, family and friends, money, and numbers.

I Want to Learn Sign Language, Volumes 1 and 2. Fort Mill, SC: American Production Services, 2001.

Led by Gallaudet University graduate Karen Green, three young girls learn basic sign language in preparation for a visit from their deaf cousin. Vocabulary is introduced by topic, and Deaf Culture and history issues are covered as well.

Number Signs for Everyone: Numbering in American Sign Language. San Diego: Dawn Pictures, 1997.

This ninety-minute videotape teaches number signs as well as appropriate use of numbers in concepts such as time, age, dollar amounts, and game scores. It includes English voice-over as well as closed captions.

Signing Time! Volume 1: My First Signs. Salt Lake City, UT: Two Little Hands Productions, 2002.

Signing Time! Volume 2: Playtime Signs. Salt Lake City, UT: Two Little Hands Productions, 2002.

Signing Time! Volume 3: Everyday Signs. Salt Lake City, UT: Two Little Hands Productions, 2002.

Signing Time! Volume 4: Family, Feelings, and Fun. Salt Lake City, UT: Two Little Hands Productions, 2004.

Signing Time! Volume 5: ABC Signs. Salt Lake City, UT: Two Little Hands Productions, 2004.

Signing Time! Volume 6: My Favorite Things. Salt Lake City, UT: Two Little Hands Productions, 2004.

Hands down the best sign language series for young children. Available on both VHS and DVD, these productions feature both hearing and deaf kids signing simple signs, along with review segments with fun songs and stories to reinforce vocabulary. Excellent segments geared to adults offer information about ASL grammar and using signs with children.

You Can Sign, Volumes 1, 2, and 3. Salem, Oreg.: Sign Enhancers, 1998.

This three-volume video series for beginning learners shows ASL being used in a natural context, with the four members of the Bravo family leading viewers through their daily lives. A narrator highlights key vocabulary for each lesson, and voice-over and closed captions make the video accessible to all. Lessons cover topics such as morning routines, meals, school signs, colors, numbers, work-related signs, and household signs.

Resources about Deaf Culture, History, and Accessibility

Americans with Disabilities Act information (www.usdoj.gov/crt/ada)

The place to go for official information about compliance with the Americans with Disabilities Act.

Disability Access Symbols project (www.gag.org/resources/das.php)

This site contains twelve symbols that can be downloaded for free or ordered on a floppy disk and used on flyers, signs, and other promotional materials to publicize accessibility of public events. Symbols include access for people with low vision, access for people in wheelchairs, audio description for the blind, TTY access, volume-control telephone, assistive listening systems, sign language interpretation, large print, information, closed captions, open captions, and braille.

Gannon, Jack R. *The Week the World Heard Gallaudet.* Washington, D.C.: Gallaudet University Press, 1989.

The Deaf President Now movement of 1988 led to the appointment of the first deaf president of Gallaudet University. Gannon's inspiring photo-history traces the week of the protest and examines the repercussions.

Groce, Nora Ellen. *Everyone Here Spoke Sign Language: Hereditary Deafness on Martha's Vineyard.* Cambridge, Mass.: Harvard University Press, 1985.

Groce's fascinating and highly readable medical-anthropological work details her research on the lost culture of Martha's Vineyard, which for two hundred years boasted such a large deaf population that nearly everyone on the island signed.

Lane, Harlan, Robert Hoffmeister, and Ben Bahan. *A Journey into the Deaf-World.* San Diego: DawnSignPress, 1996.

Written by a deaf man, a hearing child of deaf parents, and a hearing scholar renowned for his work on deaf history, this book is a comprehensive overview of the struggles and joys deaf people and American Sign Language have faced in the United States and around the world.

Moore, Matthew S., and Linda Levitan. *For Hearing People Only: Answers to Some of the Most Commonly Asked Questions about the Deaf Community, Its Culture, and the "Deaf Reality."* New York: Deaf Life Press, 1993.

This highly readable and entertaining introduction to Deaf Culture and deafness is presented in a question and answer format and covers questions as diverse as "Is there one sign language for all countries?" and "How do deaf people feel when a hearing person approaches them in public using sign language?"

Padden, Carol, and Tom Humphries. *Deaf in America: Voices from a Culture.* Cambridge, Mass.: Harvard University Press, 1988.

The two deaf authors of this classic book explore the differences between the Deaf and hearing views of deafness. An excellent introduction to Deaf Culture.

See What I Mean: Differences between Deaf and Hearing Cultures. Dallas, Tex.: Eye to Eye Productions, 2001.

"Miss Deaf Manners" and "Miss Hearing Manners" illuminate the differences between Deaf and hearing cultures on this humorous and informative video.

Willow, Morgan Grayce. *Crossing That Bridge: A Guide to Making Literary Events Accessible to Deaf and Hard-of-Hearing.* Minneapolis: SASE: Write Place, 2000.

This slim, readable volume is a singular resource for librarians, particularly in planning poetry readings and other such events geared to adults. Willow covers both events in English and those in ASL and offers detailed guidelines and checklists for hiring and working with interpreters, logistics, publicizing events, and budgeting.

Resource Books for Planning Library and Preschool Programs Using Signs

Garcia, Joseph. *Sign with Your Baby: How to Communicate with Infants before They Can Speak*. Seattle: Northlight Communications, 1999.
  With solid research to back it up, this book guides parents and other adults to effective techniques for using ASL with babies. Garcia cites the many benefits of using signs with infants and gives practical tips for when and how to introduce signs, including a guide to the most effective signs to introduce in the early months. The book also contains an illustrated glossary of 147 signs to use with young children.

Hafer, Jan C., and Robert M. Wilson. *Come Sign with Us: Sign Language Activities for Children*. Washington, D.C.: Gallaudet University Press, 2002.
  This book features twenty lessons on basic sign language, broken down into easy chunks such as "Asking Questions" and "Saying Hello." Vocabulary presented in each lesson is shown through clear line drawings, and cultural information is included in each. The lessons here could easily be adapted for a sign language program series.

Marsh, Valerie. *Beyond Words: Great Stories for Hands and Voice*. Fort Atkinson, Wis.: Highsmith, 1995.
  This collection of twenty folktales and original stories is an ideal resource for librarians to use in programming. Each story is accompanied by drawings of several signs that would be appropriate to teach to children during the telling.

Stone-Harris, Rachel. *Let's Learn about Deafness: Classroom Activities*. Washington, D.C.: Gallaudet University Press, 1988.
  This resource book features activities and worksheets appropriate for elementary-age students, focusing on Deaf Culture, terminology, basic sign language, and famous deaf people.

Warner, Penny. *Learn to Sign the Fun Way: Let Your Fingers Do the Talking with Games, Puzzles, and Activities in American Sign Language*. New York: Prima, 2001.
  The first half of this unintimidating book features kid-friendly drawings of signs organized by topic, as well as Deaf Culture information. The second half is packed with sign language games for signers at various levels, many of which could easily be used in library programs.

Books about ASL and Deafness to Share in Sign Language Programs

Ancona, George, and Mary Beth. *Handtalk Zoo*. New York: Four Winds Press, 1989.
  On a photographic trek through the zoo, a multicultural group of children demonstrates signs for animals, food, and time. What makes this book unique is its depiction of the movement of signs through blurring of the photographs. Though this means the signs are not always 100 percent understandable, it's a great way to lead into a discussion of the visual nature of ASL. Signs to use with this book: TIME, WHERE, WILL, WE, GO, THERE, ELEPHANT, LET'S, SEE, BEAR, TIGER, HORSE, ZEBRA,

THEY, FEED, SEAL, NOW, HUNGRY, numbers 1–12, LUNCH, YUMMY, JUICE, MILK, HAMBURGER, ICE-CREAM, PIZZA, POPCORN, APPLE, DOWN, YOU, NOT, MONKEY, GIRAFFE, LION, RHINOCEROS, CROCODILE, PARROT, DEER, WOLF, PENGUIN, CAN, TOUCH, ANIMAL, DUCK, RABBIT, TIRED, CLOSE, GOOD-BYE, letters A–Z

Chaplin, Susan Gibbons. *I Can Sign My ABCs*. Washington, D.C.: Gallaudet University Press, 1986.

With colorful, large illustrations, this book is perfect for introducing the manual alphabet in programs. It also contains a sign for a word beginning with each letter of the alphabet, which expands its usefulness considerably. Use in alphabet programs or to highlight specific signs in any program. Signs to use with this book: letters A–Z, APPLE, BALL, CAT, DOG, EYE, FLOWER, GLASS, HAT, I, JACKET, KEY, LIGHT, MILK, NOSE, ORANGE, PIG, QUEEN, RABBIT, SHOES, TREE, UMBRELLA, VALENTINE, WINDOW, XYLOPHONE, YO-YO, ZIPPER

Charlip, Remy, Mary Beth, and George Ancona. *Handtalk Birthday: A Number and Story Book in Sign Language*. New York: Four Winds Press, 1987.

The female protagonist of this story is wakened by her flashing doorbell, only to find that her friends have come to surprise her for her birthday. The story is told through photos depicting people signing, along with English translations of the signs. As in *Handtalk Zoo*, the photos depict the movement of the signs. Signs to use with this story: WHO, WHAT, WHERE, WHEN, WHY, SURPRISE, WOW, COME-IN, INSIDE, GUESS, BALL, NO, DRUM, CAN, FISH, BIG, TELL, ME, GIVE-UP, OPEN, HAT, THANK-YOU, SNAKE, TELESCOPE, BAT, HOT-DOG, STOP, CRAZY, MATCH, MY, MORE, RING, BOOK, CAT, ROLLER-SKATE, GLOVE, WATCH, RADIO, ROBOT, TV, PARTY, CANDY, CHEWING-GUM, PUNCH, CAKE, COOKIE, HAPPY, BIRTHDAY, YOU, DEAR, MAKE, WISH, CAREFUL, OLD, numbers 1–22, 33, 44, 55, 66, 77, 88, 99, 100, 200, 1,000, SECRET, GOOD-BYE

Early Sign Language: An Alphabet of Animal Signs. Eugene, Oreg.: Garlic Press, 2002.

Early Sign Language: First Signs. Eugene, Oreg.: Garlic Press, 2002.

Early Sign Language: Food Signs. Eugene, Oreg.: Garlic Press, 2002.

Early Sign Language: Signs for Pets and Animals. Eugene, Oreg.: Garlic Press, 2002.

Each of these board books uses full-color photos of the objects, plus colorful line drawings depicting the sign for each. Though the illustrations may be too small for group sharing, these books could be adapted to a storycard format or used as a programming resource for learning signs on a particular topic. Signs to use with these books:

An Alphabet of Animal Signs: ALLIGATOR, BEAR, CAT, DOG, ELEPHANT, FROG, GIRAFFE, HORSE, INSECT, JAY, KANGAROO, LION, MONKEY, NEWT, OWL, PARROT, QUAIL, RABBIT, SHEEP, TIGER, UNICORN, VULTURE, WOLF, OX, YAK, ZEBRA, letters A–Z

First Signs: BABY, MOTHER, FATHER, PLEASE, THANK-YOU, DRINK, EAT/FOOD, FINISH, MORE, BANANA, APPLE, COOKIE, MILK, HELP, HURT, GO, STOP, BALL, BOOK, CAT, DOG, CAR/TRUCK, AIRPLANE, TOILET, BATH, BED, PLAY, I-LOVE-YOU

Food Signs: EAT/FOOD, APPLE, BACON, BANANA, BERRY, BREAD, BROC-
COLI, CABBAGE, CAKE, CANDY, CARROT, CEREAL, CHEESE, CHERRY,
CHICKEN, CHIPS, COOKIE, CORN, EGG, FISH, FRENCH-FRIES, FRUIT,
GRAPES, HAMBURGER, HOT-DOG, ICE-CREAM, JUICE, LEMON, LETTUCE,
MACARONI, MEAT, MELON, MILK, MUFFIN, NUT, ORANGE, PANCAKE,
PEACH, PEAR, PEAS, PINEAPPLE, POPCORN, POTATO, RICE, SALAD, SAND-
WICH, SOUP, SPAGHETTI, SPINACH, STRAWBERRY, TOAST, TURKEY, VEG-
ETABLE

Signs for Pets and Animals: PET, CAT, DOG, MOUSE, RABBIT, BIRD, TURTLE,
FISH, FROG, DUCK, COW, HORSE, SHEEP, PIG, SQUIRREL, BEAR, ELE-
PHANT, MONKEY, LION, TIGER, CAMEL, ALLIGATOR, SPIDER, SNAKE,
KANGAROO

Fain, Kathleen. *Handsigns: A Sign Language Alphabet.* San Francisco: Chronicle, 1993.
This book presents a large color illustration of an animal for each letter of the alphabet,
along with the corresponding letter of the manual alphabet. Though the signs for the
animals themselves are not included, this is a unique way to introduce the manual
alphabet. Signs to use with this story: letters A–Z

Golder, Stephen, and Lise Memling. *Buffy's Orange Leash.* Washington, D.C.: Gallaudet
University Press, 1988.
Buffy is a hearing dog who lives with the Johnson family. Because Mr. and Mrs. Johnson are deaf, it is Buffy's job to let them know when the doorbell rings, the fire alarm
goes off, or when their baby is crying. The story describes Buffy's selection and training
as a hearing dog and how he fits into the Johnson family's life. Though the book is a
bit old (it contains a reference to TDDs, or telecommunication devices for the deaf,
while the more acceptable term now is TTY, or teletypewriter), the information presented about hearing dogs remains solid. Signs to use with this book: DEAF, DOG,
HEAR

Kelley, Walter P. *Victory Week.* Rochester, New York: Deaf Life Press, 1998.
In language accessible to younger children, a child narrator tells the story of the 1988
Deaf President Now movement at Gallaudet University, which resulted in the appoint-
ment of Gallaudet's first deaf president. Signs to use with this book: SCHOOL, UNI-
VERSITY, DEAF, PRESIDENT, NOW, STUDENT, TEACHER, SIGN, APPLAUD

Lakin, Patricia. *Dad and Me in the Morning.* New York: Whitman, 1994.
Jacob, a young deaf boy, wakes early to the flashing of his special alarm clock. He wakes
his father, and they walk down to the beach. This poetic story is beautifully illustrated
in glowing watercolors and is an ideal discussion starter about deafness for preschool
and elementary programs. Signs to use with this book: HEARING-AID, FATHER,
SIGNING, RABBIT, MORNING, COLD, BIRD, SUN

Lee, Jeanne. *Silent Lotus.* New York: Farrar, Straus, and Giroux, 1991.
This story depicts a young deaf girl growing up in twelfth-century Cambodia; though
she is deaf and cannot communicate with her parents, she quickly blossoms when she
becomes a dancer at court. With large, simple illustrations, this story adds a unique
multicultural dimension to discussions of deafness and is a great lead-in to discussing

deaf people throughout history. Signs to use with this story: BABY, DEAF, MOTHER, FATHER, DANCE

Millman, Isaac. *Moses Goes to the Circus*. New York: Farrar, Straus, and Giroux, 2003. Moses, a young deaf boy, goes to the circus with his hearing family in this excellent picture book. Sidebars teach signs related to the story, and kids will recognize themselves in Moses's interactions with his little sister. A wonderful story for teaching animal signs or discussing families. Signs to use with this story: I, GO, CIRCUS, CAT, HAVE, WHISKERS, ELEPHANT, TRUNK, SIT, FRONT, 2, DOG, ON, SEESAW, TRAPEZE-ARTIST, FLY-THROUGH-AIR, MY, SISTER, LOVE, ICE-CREAM, ASSISTANT, CLOWN, WEAR, CLOWN-NOSE, LIKE, WITH, JUGGLER, ACRO-BAT, MAGICIAN, HORSE, GRAND, PARADE

Millman, Isaac. *Moses Goes to a Concert*. New York: Farrar, Straus, and Giroux, 1998. The first book in the *Moses* series, this picture book follows Moses and his deaf classmates as they attend a concert. They have a chance to meet a percussionist in the orchestra, who is deaf, and the story deals with the ways deaf people enjoy music through vibrations. This is a wonderful story to use with any deaf awareness program, especially to discuss the idea that deaf people can do just about anything that hearing people can do. For a great extension activity, play music loudly and give each child a balloon to hold in his or her lap, as the deaf children do in the story. Signs to use with this story: I, PLAY, DRUM, TEACHER, HAVE, SURPRISE, MY, FRIEND, LOUD, MUSIC, SOUND, WE, WAVE, APPLAUD, 11, BEAUTIFUL, BALLOON, FEEL, VIBRATION, FRIEND, DEAF, WORK, HEART, GOAL, BECOME, PERCUSSION-IST, AND, SUCCEED, THANK-YOU, GOOD-BYE, SO-MUCH, FUN, WHEN, YOU, SET-YOUR-MIND, CAN, ANYTHING, WANT, GROW-UP, DOCTOR, ARTIST, LAWYER, FARMER, ELECTRICIAN, ACTOR, letters A–Z

Millman, Isaac. *Moses Goes to School*. New York: Farrar, Straus, and Giroux, 2000. One of the best picture books on the market today depicting deaf kids, this story follows Moses, a young deaf boy, through his day at a school for the deaf. Like the other books in the series, this book combines a simple story with drawings of signs. This book is especially useful for launching discussions of the similarities and differences between deaf and hearing people, and readers even learn about the differences between ASL and English as Moses writes to his hearing pen pal. A wonderful book to use with preschool, elementary, and even middle school audiences. The book also contains instructions for signing the song "Take Me Out to the Ball Game." Signs to use with this book: I, GO, DEAF, SCHOOL, NEW, BABY, SISTER, MY, FRIEND, WEAR, HEARING-AID, WRITE, LETTER, CLASS, WE, STAND, HAPPY, LIVE, APARTMENT, LOVE, DOG

Millman, Isaac. *Moses Sees a Play*. New York: Farrar, Straus, and Giroux, 2004. This Moses adventure focuses on theater, as actors from the Little Theatre of the Deaf visit Moses's school to perform "Cinderella." A class of hearing students from another nearby school joins Moses and his friends for the play, and Moses quickly befriends a boy named Manuel, who has recently moved to the United States and knows neither English nor American Sign Language. This is a wonderful story for discussing communication and relations between deaf and hearing people, friendship, and the role of the theater in the deaf community. Like the other books in the series, this book combines a story with line drawings that teach signs. This book lends itself especially well to extension activities involving gestures and acting out favorite fairy tales. Signs to use with this book: WE, HAVE, VISITOR, LITTLE, THEATER, DEAF, I, EIGHT-YEARS-OLD, EAT/FOOD, LUNCH, MEAN, STEPMOTHER, STEPSISTER, OTHER, PRINCE, FAIRY-GODMOTHER, HORSE, CARRIAGE, LIKE, FAIRY-TALE, ELEPHANT, BIG, ANIMAL, CAMEL, LIVE, DESERT, MET, NEW, FRIEND, SEE, SCHOOL, ALSO, HE, HEARS, COMMUNICATE, USE, GESTURE, MY, SPECIAL

Rankin, Laura. *The Handmade Alphabet*. New York: Dial Books, 1991.

This lyrical interpretation of the manual alphabet combines the handshapes with illustrations of related objects—a beautiful way to introduce ASL letters and an ideal springboard for a craft encouraging children to create their own versions of the illustrations using clip-art handshapes. Signs to use with this book: letters A–Z

Rankin, Laura. *The Handmade Counting Book*. New York: Dial Books, 1998.

This book features beautiful illustrations of the handshapes for specific numbers, each accompanied by the English language numeral and an illustration showing a corresponding number of objects. It's a great way to introduce the basic number handshapes to any age group. Signs to use with this book: numbers 1–20, 25, 50, 75, 100

Riggio, Anita. *Secret Signs: Along the Underground Railroad*. Honesdale, Pa.: Boyds Mill Press, 1997.

In the mid-1800s, Luke and his mother help support themselves by making panoramic eggs of maple sugar. When a man bursts into their home and accuses them of hiding slaves, Luke's mother denies the charges, although she is planning to meet her contact on the Underground Railroad that very day. With his mother held at home, Luke, who is deaf, must use his resources and creative talents to make the connection. This is a wonderful picture book to use with elementary-age children and teenagers and is most notable because it presents a deaf character that is a person first, rather than a stereotype. Signs to use with this story: MOTHER, DEAF, EGG, PAINT, BRAVE

Slier, Debby. *Animal Signs: A First Book of Sign Language*. New York: Checkerboard Press, 1995.

Slier, Debby. *Word Signs: A First Book of Sign Language*. New York: Checkerboard Press, 1993.

Though the line drawings depicting the signs in these board books are far too small for sharing with storytime groups, the bright and colorful photos are ideal, and the presenter could use the line drawings to refresh his or her memory while demonstrating the signs. Signs to use with these books:

Animal Signs: SHEEP, DUCK, TURTLE, GOAT, CAT, FISH, DOG, RABBIT, ROOSTER, FROG, COW, MOUSE

Word Signs: SOCKS, CRAYONS, BOWL, CRACKER, CUP, BABY, FLOWER, BALL, SHOES, BOOK, HAT, BEAR

Uhlberg, Myron. *The Printer*. Atlanta: Peachtree, 2003.

A young boy tells the story of his deaf father, who works in a printing plant. One day, when fire overtakes the plant, the boy's father and the other deaf printers are able to save the lives of all the men inside, who don't hear the fire over the roar of the printing presses. An inspiring and beautiful picture book, ideal for sharing with all ages, that also depicts an important part of Deaf Culture. Signs to use with this book: FATHER, NEWSPAPER, HAT, DEAF, HEARING-PERSON, WORK, SIGN, FIRE, THANK-YOU

Votry, Kim. *Baby's First Signs.* Washington, D.C.: Gallaudet University Press, 2001.

Votry, Kim. *A Book of Colors.* Washington, D.C.: Gallaudet University Press, 2003.

Votry, Kim. *More Baby's First Signs.* Washington, D.C.: Gallaudet University Press, 2001.

Votry, Kim. *Out for a Walk.* Washington, D.C.: Gallaudet University Press, 2003.

Using bold illustrations of everyday objects and activities, these bright board books in the *Baby's First Sign* series introduce basic baby signs through clear pencil drawings. These books are ideal for introducing signs in baby programs and could easily be translated into storycard format if their small size does not work for larger audiences. Also consider using these books to highlight specific signs in programs for any age group. Signs to use with these books:

Baby's First Signs: MILK, EAT/FOOD, BATH, CHANGE, SOCKS, BIRD, MORE, LIGHT, FATHER, MOTHER, MOON, BOOK, SHOES, PLAY

A Book of Colors: COLOR, RED, ORANGE, YELLOW, GREEN, BLUE, PURPLE, PINK, TAN, BROWN, BLACK, WHITE, GRAY, RAINBOW

More Baby's First Signs: BALL, FLOWER, HOT, BED, TREE, CAR/TRUCK, WATER, BLANKET, COLD, RAIN, BABY, AIRPLANE, DONE, WIND

Out for a Walk: OUTSIDE, WALK, SEE, BUTTERFLY, HEAR, DOG, SMELL, TASTE, CAT, TOUCH, FRIEND, JUMP, SQUIRREL, HOME

Wheeler, Cindy. *More Simple Signs.* New York: Viking, 1998.

Like *Simple Signs*, this book features a colorful illustration depicting a concept on each page, along with a line drawing showing the sign for that concept and a hint to help remember the sign. This book is a wonderful way to teach simple signs in a program focusing on ASL, or a great supplement to highlight a few signs in any program. The book also features exceptionally clear illustrations of the manual alphabet on the endpapers. Signs to use with this book: letters A–Z, SUN, BOY, GIRL, PLAY, JUMP, SIT, SWING, APPLE, TREE, RED, BLUE, YELLOW, GREEN, FISH, HORSE, MONKEY, TIGER, AIRPLANE, LOUD, YES, NO, STOP, GO, HURT, HELP, PLEASE, THANK-YOU, HOUSE, RAIN, RAINBOW

Wheeler, Cindy. *Simple Signs.* New York: Puffin, 1995.

With color illustrations of each concept and line drawings depicting sign production, along with a helpful hint for remembering each sign, this book of basic signs is a great supplement to sign language programs. Use the whole book to introduce multiple signs, or choose specific pages to highlight and reinforce particular signs in your program. Signs to use with this book: HELLO, CAT, DOG, BALL, CAR/TRUCK, MILK, BANANA, COOKIE, EAT, MORE, FINISH, HAPPY, CRY, BOOK, MUSIC, BABY, MOTHER, FATHER, BIRD, COW, BUTTERFLY, TURTLE, SNAKE, ELEPHANT, FRIEND, BICYCLE, MOON, SLEEP, LOVE

Winnie-the-Pooh's ABC: Sign Language Edition. New York: Dutton, 2001.
This book features the manual alphabet, along with a sign corresponding to a word beginning with each letter. The illustrations by Ernest Shepherd are a bit small for storytime sharing, as are the line drawings of the signs, but this book would work well with smaller groups or to highlight specific signs in a storycard format. Signs to use with this book: letters A–Z, APPLE, BALLOON, COW, DRAGON, DONKEY, FOR-EST, GATE, HONEY, ISLAND, JUMP, KANGAROO, LION, MIRROR, NORTH, OWL, PIG, QUEEN, RABBIT, STAIRS, TIGER, UMBRELLA, PURPLE, FLOWER, BEAR, LOOK-FOR, YELLOW, numbers 1–10

Annotated Bibliography of Materials to Use with Sign Language

All books and albums listed here are recommended in at least one of the sample programs. This section includes specific suggestions for creating props, extending the stories, and incorporating signs. In many cases, multiple signs are suggested for use with the stories, including many signs in addition to those found in appendix E. Consult a resource person or one of the resources found in appendix A to learn these signs. You may want to focus on only a few signs with each story or song, depending on the topic of your program. See chapters 4 and 5 for more specific guidelines for choosing signs to use in your programs.

A note about adapting books: Many of these books are easy to shorten by clipping pages together with paper clips. If you want to focus only on specific signs, or if you can't find some of the signs, feel free to skip some.

Picture Books

Arnold, Caroline. *Playtime for Zoo Animals*. Minneapolis: Carolrhoda Books, 1999.
This simple nonfiction book is just right for introducing animal signs to young children. Crisp photos and a brief text make this a good storytime choice. Signs to use with this story: PLAY, MONKEY, ELEPHANT, LION, BIRD, TIGER, BEAR, SEAL, HIPPO-POTAMUS

Arnosky, Jim. *Rabbits and Raindrops*. New York: Putnam, 1997.
With beautiful color-splashed illustrations and a large format, this picture book follows Mother Rabbit and her five babies as they explore the field and then find cover from the rain. This gentle story is wonderful to use with any age group from toddlers on up. Signs to use with this story: RABBIT, MOTHER, SUN, BABY, BEE, RAIN, BUT-TERFLY, RAINBOW, PLAY

Asch, Frank. *Good Night, Baby Bear*. San Diego: Harcourt, 1998.
It's time to hibernate for the winter, but Baby Bear simply can't get to sleep. This is a tender, simple story, perfect for toddler, preschool, and family programs. Signs to use with this story: BABY, MOTHER, BEAR, SLEEP, WINTER, APPLE, WATER, MOON, KISS, GOOD-NIGHT

Asch, Frank. *Just Like Daddy*. New York: Simon & Schuster, 1981.
Little Bear wants to do everything just like his daddy, including picking a flower for his mother—but in the end he catches a fish, just like . . . Mommy. A lovely book with a funny twist ending for toddler, preschool, and family programs. Signs to use with this story: BEAR, FATHER, MOTHER, SAME, EAT/FOOD, FISHING, FLOWER, WORM, FISH

Asquith, Ros. *Ball!* New York: DK, 1999.
This simple book from the *Toddler Play Book* series features a ball on a string that can be bounced in and out of each picture as the baby chases it through the story. The simple text features lots of repetition (the perfect place to reinforce signs) and silly language. Signs to use with this story: BABY, BALL, RED, MOTHER

Axtell, David. *We're Going on a Lion Hunt*. New York: Henry Holt, 1999.
This fun rendition of the popular "Goin' on a Bear Hunt" features two sisters looking for a different animal on the African savannah. This fun, interactive story with actions built in would work well either as a read-aloud or as a flannelboard telling. Signs to use with this story: LION, SCARED, GIRAFFE, SWIM, DARK, ELEPHANT, TIRED

Bajaj, Varsha. *How Many Kisses Do You Want Tonight?* New York: Little, Brown, 2004.
It's bedtime, and the parents of a little boy, a little girl, and various forest animals ask how many kisses their children want. This warm and simple bedtime book is great for toddler and family programs. Signs to use with this story: numbers 1–10, KISS, FATHER, BEAR, BABY, MOTHER, DUCK, CAT, BUTTERFLY, HORSE, DOG, BIRD, SNAKE, RABBIT, GIRL, BOY, 100, MILLION

Baker, Alan. *Little Rabbits' First Farm Book*. New York: Kingfisher, 2001.
The little rabbits help out on the farm, feeding the chickens and ducks and even driving the tractor and milking the cows. A simple story is combined with "Did You Know?" segments on the right-hand side of the page offering very easy farm facts. This book could be used as just a story, just a nonfiction book, or as both. Signs to use with this story: RABBIT, ROOSTER, FARM, CHICKEN, EGG, BABY, DUCK, COW, PIG, SHEEP, DRIVE, APPLE, TREE, MILK, EAT/FOOD, GOOD-NIGHT

Bang, Molly. *Ten, Nine, Eight*. New York: Greenwillow, 1983.
This classic bedtime story counts down from ten to one as a little African American girl goes to bed. Perfect for any age storytime, this book could be used as a read-aloud or adapted to a flannelboard format. Signs to use with this story: numbers 1–10, BED

Barry, Frances. *Duckie's Rainbow*. Cambridge, Mass.: Candlewick, 2004.
The unique rainbow shape and die-cut pages of this picture book are a perfect way to introduce color signs. As Duckie walks home she encounters the various colors of the rainbow, and each turn of the page creates another stripe of color at the top of the book, until Duckie looks up and sees the beautiful rainbow above. The text is simple

enough for toddlers, yet the unique design of the book will capture the interest of older kids as well. Signs to use with this story: DUCK, RED, ORANGE, YELLOW, GREEN, BLUE, PURPLE, RAINBOW

Berry, Holly. *Old MacDonald Had a Farm*. New York: North-South Books, 1994.

With large, bright, clean illustrations of animals frolicking on the farm, this book is a wonderful way to present or supplement the classic song. Signs to use with this story: FARM, PIG, CAT, COW, CHICKEN, DONKEY, DUCK, DOG, SHEEP

Bornstein, Ruth Lercher. *Rabbit's Good News*. New York: Clarion, 1995.

Rabbit leaves her family sleeping in their warm dark burrow and follows the something that softly calls to her, just in time to find out that spring has arrived. Signs to use with this story: RABBIT, SLEEP, FLOWER, WORM, BIRD, BUTTERFLY, SPRING

Breeze, Lynn. *Pickle and the Ball*. New York: Kingfisher, 1998.

This simple board book shows baby Pickle playing with a ball in various ways. The bright illustrations and simple rhyming text are perfect for baby storytimes, and this book adapts very well to a storycard format if the size is too small for your audience. Signs to use with this story: BALL, BEAR, CHAIR, PLAY

Breeze, Lynn. *Pickle and the Blocks*. New York: Kingfisher, 1998.

This smaller-format board book may be too small for storytime on its own, but the simple story and charming illustrations are perfect for an enlarged storycard or even retelling using a doll and a bunch of blocks. Signs to use with this story: YELLOW, BLUE, RED, PLAY

Bridwell, Norman. *Clifford Counts Bubbles*. New York: Scholastic, 1992.

Clifford the small red puppy follows the bubbles as they float along, counting them as they land on a cat, a rabbit, a butterfly, and some mice. Though this board book is too small for sharing on its own, it adapts well to a flannelboard or prop story. Signs to use with this story: numbers 1–10, CAT, RABBIT, MOUSE, BUTTERFLY

Bridwell, Norman. *Clifford's Bathtime*. New York: Scholastic, 1991.

Clifford the small red puppy has an adventure in the tub when he falls off a bar of soap, but rubber duckie comes to his rescue. This small board book is too small for storytime sharing, but the simple story translates well to a storycard, prop story, or flannelboard retelling. Signs to use with this story: WASH, MOTHER, DUCK, PLAY

Bridwell, Norman. *Clifford's First Autumn*. New York: Scholastic, 1997.

Clifford the small red puppy jumps in a leaf pile, upsets a cart of pumpkins, and gets himself involved in a football game. Signs to use with this story: DOG, BIRD, LEAF, PUMPKIN, WIND, FOOTBALL

Bridwell, Norman. *Clifford's First Valentine's Day*. New York: Scholastic, 1997.

Clifford the small red puppy gets into all kinds of trouble as Emily Elizabeth gets ready for Valentine's Day. Signs to use with this story: DOG, VALENTINE/HEART, DAY, HAPPY, HELP, GLUE, RED, MAIL

Brisson, Pat. *Benny's Pennies*. New York: Doubleday, 1993.

Benny McBride has five pennies, and he spends each on something to make one of his family members happy. This wonderfully simple story for teaching number signs, family signs, and more works well with toddler, preschool, and family programs. For a simple flannelboard rendition of this story, print out large clip-art pictures of five pennies and the objects that Benny buys. This would also make a wonderful audience participation story, with children playing the parts of the different characters. Signs to use with this story: numbers 1–5, CENT, MOTHER, BROTHER, SISTER, CAT, DOG, BUY, FLOWER, COOKIE, HAT, BONE, FISH, THANK-YOU

Brown, Craig. *In the Spring.* New York: Greenwillow, 1994.

Spring on the farm means the arrival of many new baby animals, including twins for the farmer's wife. Signs to use with this story: SPRING, BABY, SHEEP, CAT, COW, PIG, GOAT, CHICKEN, DUCK, HORSE

Brown, Marc. *D. W. All Wet.* Boston: Little, Brown, 1988.

D. W. does nothing but complain when she and her family go to the beach, but once her brother tricks her into going into the water, she has so much fun she doesn't want to leave. Signs to use with this story: HOT, OCEAN, WALK, PLAY

Brown, Margaret Wise. *Goodnight Moon.* New York: Harper and Row, 1947.

This classic bedtime book is easily enhanced by signs and adapts well to a flannelboard format. Signs to use with this story: GOOD-NIGHT, MOON, TELEPHONE, RED, BALLOON, COW, BEAR, CAT, MOUSE, STAR

Brown, Margaret Wise. *My World of Color.* New York: Hyperion, 2002.

Rhyming verses describe the many colors in our world, while oversized illustrations by Loretta Krupinski make this book ideal for storytime sharing. The rhyming text could also be used with a flannelboard rendition. Signs to use with this story: RED, ORANGE, YELLOW, GREEN, BLUE, PURPLE, BROWN, BLACK, GRAY, WHITE, PINK

Bruce, Lisa. *Fran's Flower.* New York: HarperCollins, 1999.

Fran grows frustrated with the flower she's trying to grow and throws the pot outside . . . but nature takes its course and eventually a beautiful flower grows there anyway. Signs to use with this story: FLOWER, DOG, FOOD, PIZZA, CHEESE, HAMBURGER, SPAGHETTI, COOKIE, ICE-CREAM, BONE, RAIN, WIND, SUN

Burningham, John. *Mr. Gumpy's Motor Car.* New York: HarperCollins, 1973.

Mr. Gumpy and his friends enjoy a lovely ride—until it starts to rain. This story is a fun read-aloud for family programs and would work well as a flannelboard or a prop story told with a toy car and stuffed animals. Be sure to get out your squirt bottle for the rainy parts. Signs to use with this story: CAR/TRUCK, RABBIT, CAT, DOG, PIG, SHEEP, CHICKEN, COW, GOAT, RAIN, SUN, SWIM, GOOD-BYE.

Butler, John. *Whose Nose and Toes?* New York: Viking, 2004.

With simple illustrations and an easy question and answer text, this book invites little ones to guess the identity of several animals based on the nose and toes shown on the page. Signs to use with this story: TIGER, PIG, DUCK, RHINOCEROS, GIRAFFE, DOG, MONKEY, COW, CROCODILE, ELEPHANT

Butterworth, Nick. *Jasper's Beanstalk.* New York: Simon & Schuster, 1993.

With a simple text and lots of bright, bold illustrations by Mick Inkpen, this book is ideal for sharing with younger children and family groups. It makes a great stick puppet story as well. Even if you don't have time to make elaborate props, consider photocopying and enlarging the beanstalk at the end of the story. When you reach that point in the story, show the beanstalk growing over the top of the book. Signs to use with this story: WATER, days of the week

Cabrera, Jane. *Cat's Colors*. New York: Dial, 1997.

Cat explores the colors, finally deciding that orange is his favorite—because it's the color of his mother's fur. With large, bold illustrations and a brief text, this story is perfect for storytimes with younger children. Signs to use with this story: CAT, GREEN, PINK, BLACK, RED, YELLOW, PURPLE, BROWN, BLUE, WHITE, ORANGE, MOTHER

Camp, Lindsay. *The Biggest Bed in the World*. New York: HarperCollins, 1999.

A father tries to solve the problem of his whole family wanting to sleep in the same bed by building increasingly larger beds, until the largest falls right out of the house and rolls to the sea. Preschoolers, elementary-age kids, and families will love this silly picture book, and it's a great way to introduce family signs. Signs to use with this story: BABY, MOTHER, FATHER, BED, BROTHER, SISTER, BIG, FAMILY

Campbell, Rod. *Dear Zoo*. New York: Simon & Schuster, 1982.

A child writes to the zoo for a pet, but each one they send isn't quite right, until a puppy arrives. The lift-the-flap format and simple storyline make this book ideal for using with younger children, and the addition of animal signs will hook older kids as well. For additional fun, try telling this as a prop story using stuffed animals in boxes marked "From the Zoo" and "Danger," like the crates in the book. Signs to use with this story: ELEPHANT, GIRAFFE, LION, CAMEL, SNAKE, MONKEY, FROG, DOG

Capucilli, Alyssa Satin. *Bathtime for Biscuit*. New York: HarperCollins, 1998.

With charming illustrations and a simple, repetitive text, this beginning reader is also a great read-aloud for baby and toddler storytimes. Use a towel to act out the puppies' tug-of-war, and spray a water bottle when the little girl splashes into the tub. Signs to use with this story: WASH, DOG

Carle, Eric. *Do You Want to Be My Friend?* New York: HarperCollins, 1976.

Sign language is an ideal way to support this nearly wordless picture book. A little mouse is looking for a friend but doesn't find one until he approaches another mouse. Signs to use with this story: FRIEND, MOUSE, HORSE, BIRD, CROCODILE, LION, RHINOCEROS, SEAL, MONKEY, PEACOCK, FOX, KANGAROO, GIRAFFE, SNAKE, YES

Carle, Eric. *From Head to Toe*. New York: HarperCollins, 1997.

This movement-based picture book invites readers to imitate the actions of several unusual animals. Supplement the movements by teaching the signs as well. This is a great stretch activity during any storytime. Signs to use with this story: PENGUIN, GIRAFFE, BUFFALO, MONKEY, SEAL, GORILLA, CAT, CROCODILE, CAMEL, DONKEY, ELEPHANT, BIRD, CAN

Carle, Eric. *1, 2, 3 to the Zoo: A Counting Book*. New York: Philomel, 1968.

Sign language is a great way to present this wordless picture book. Use the story to emphasize animal signs, number signs, or both. This book adapts well to any audience.

Signs to use with this story: TRAIN, ELEPHANT, HIPPOPOTAMUS, GIRAFFE, LION, BEAR, CROCODILE, SEAL, MONKEY, SNAKE, BIRD, numbers 1–10

Carle, Eric. *Today Is Monday*. New York: Philomel, 1993.

Carle's trademark art style marks this book of days of the week, foods, and animals. Because of the minimal text and large illustrations, this book is ideal for using with signs. The book also contains music for the song on which it is based. Signs to use with this story: days of the week, GREEN, BEAN, SPAGHETTI, SOUP, MEAT, FISH, CHICKEN, ICE-CREAM, HUNGRY, PORCUPINE, SNAKE, ELEPHANT, CAT, BIRD, FOX, MONKEY

Carle, Eric. *The Very Hungry Caterpillar*. New York: Philomel, 1979.

Carle's classic picture book is great for programs about bugs, days of the week, numbers, or foods. This book adapts well to a flannelboard and is also available in a big-book format. Signs to use with this story: CATERPILLAR, HUNGRY, days of the week, numbers 1–5, APPLE, BERRY, ORANGE, CAKE, ICE-CREAM, CHEESE, PIE, WATERMELON, BUTTERFLY

Carroll, Kathleen Sullivan. *One Red Rooster*. Boston: Houghton Mifflin, 1992.

This counting book could be used to teach numbers, farm animals, or colors. With bright illustrations and a rhythmic, rhyming text, it's a perfect read-aloud for toddler and family programs. Signs to use with this story: numbers 1–10, ROOSTER, COW, BIRD, SHEEP, CAT, DOG, HORSE, DONKEY, PIG, RED, BLACK, BLUE, WHITE, ORANGE, GOLD, BROWN, GRAY, YELLOW, PINK

Chapman, Cheryl. *Snow on Snow on Snow*. New York: Dial, 1994.

Repetitive text and bright color-blocked illustrations tell the story of an African American boy and his friends' adventures in the snow. Signs to use with this story: WINTER, BLANKET, FOOD, CLOTHES, SNOW, FRIEND, SLED, TREE, LOOK-FOR, CRY, DOG

Cousins, Lucy. *Maisy Goes Swimming*. Boston: Little, Brown, 1990.

Maisy the mouse is going swimming, but first she has to remove her hat, scarf, boots, and undies and get into her bathing suit. This lift-the-flap, pull-the-tab book is great for introducing color and clothing signs and can be easily adapted to a flannelboard story. Signs to use with this story: MOUSE, BLUE, HAT, SHOES, BROWN, RED, COAT, GRAY, GREEN, PANTS, YELLOW, SOCKS, ORANGE, RAINBOW, SWIM, CLOTHES

Cousins, Lucy. *Maisy Takes a Bath*. Cambridge, Mass.: Candlewick Press, 2000.

Maisy and her friend Tallulah play in the bathtub. With large, bright illustrations and a simple text, this is a great read-aloud for baby and toddler programs. Signs to use with this story: WASH, DUCK, PLAY

Cousins, Lucy. *Maisy's Rainbow Dream*. Cambridge, Mass.: Candlewick, 2003.

Maisy dreams of taking a journey with her friends and seeing the many colors of the rainbow. With an oversized format and lots of bright, bold illustrations, this is an ideal book for introducing colors in storytime. Signs to use with this story: MOUSE, SLEEP, FRIEND, RED, ORANGE, YELLOW, GREEN, BLUE, PURPLE, RAINBOW, BEAUTIFUL, WAKE-UP

Cowley, Joy. *Mrs. Wishy-Washy*. New York: Philomel, 1999.

Mrs. Wishy-Washy washes all her farm animals in her big metal tub, but the animals just go right back into the mud. This very simple story is easy enough for baby programs and humorous enough for family programs. It would be great for bathtime or farm animal themes and would also adapt well to a flannelboard or prop story with stuffed animals. Signs to use with this story: COW, PIG, DUCK, DIRTY, WASH

Creech, Sharon. *A Fine, Fine School*. New York: HarperCollins, 2001.

Mr. Keene, a principal, loves his school so much that he decides the students should come every day, including weekends and holidays and through the summer—until one young girl educates him about too much of a good thing. Elementary school students will delight in this over-the-top tale. Teach the signs for WONDERFUL SCHOOL and have the audience sign it with you each time Mr. Keene repeats the phrase "fine, fine school." Signs to use with this story: SCHOOL, PROUD, LEARN, SUMMER, STUDENT, WONDERFUL, days of the week

Crews, Donald. *Ten Black Dots*. New York: Greenwillow, 1986.

This classic, simple counting book about the many things that black dots can represent is perfect for a read-aloud, for a simple flannelboard story, or for encouraging young children to come up with ideas of their own. The visual nature of this book makes it a perfect companion to sign language programs and a natural complement to discussion of the importance of using our eyes. Signs to use with this story: numbers 1–10

Crews, Nina. *One Hot Summer Day*. New York: Greenwillow, 1995.

With slightly surreal photo collages, this book describes a hot summer day in the city. A fun read-aloud for preschool and family programs. Signs to use with this story: SUMMER, HOT, EGG, PLAY, POPSICLE, RAIN, DANCE

Dee, Ruby. *Two Ways to Count to Ten: A Liberian Folktale*. New York: Henry Holt, 1988.

King Leopard decides to hold a contest to name his successor: whichever animal can throw a spear high enough to count to ten before it lands will be the next king. One by one, the biggest, strongest animals fail, until the antelope proves his cleverness by counting by twos. This witty folktale is great for teaching animal signs and counting signs, as well as for multicultural programs. Signs to use with this story: numbers 1–10, LEOPARD, ELEPHANT, MONKEY, LION, KING

Edwards, Pamela Duncan. *Rosie's Roses*. New York: HarperCollins, 2003.

Rosie has four roses for her aunt's birthday, but she winds up giving them away to other animals one by one, until she has only a pretty ribbon left. This is a good story for introducing simple color and number signs, as well as for birthday and flower storytimes. Signs to use with this story: AUNT, BIRTHDAY, numbers 1–4, FLOWER, RIBBON, ORANGE, RAT, BUG, RABBIT, PURPLE, TREE, BIRD, RED, WHITE, SQUIRREL

Ehlert, Lois. *Snowballs*. San Diego: Harcourt Brace, 1995.

Ehlert's photo collages depict a snow family built by a group of children. This book is ideal for toddler, preschool, and family programs about winter, or to introduce family signs. Signs to use with this story: SNOW, BIRD, FATHER, MOTHER, BOY, GIRL, BABY, CAT, DOG, SUN, MELT, GOOD-BYE

Elting, Mary, and Michael Folsom. *Q Is for Duck: An Alphabet Guessing Game*. New York: Clarion, 1980.

With charming illustrations by Jack Kent, this guessing game poses questions such as "A is for Zoo. Why?" and invites kids to guess how the letters and items are related. (A is for *zoo* because of all the animals there, of course.) This is an unusual twist on the standard alphabet book and is a great way to involve your audience in the program. Signs to use with this story: letters A–Z, WHY

Ernst, Lisa Campbell. *The Letters Are Lost*. New York: Viking, 1996.

The letters of the alphabet, as embodied by wooden blocks, go on various letter-appropriate adventures: B tumbles into the bath, D becomes a dog toy, and so on. Ernst's illustrations are large and colorful enough for storytime sharing. Signs to use with this story: letters A–Z, AIRPLANE, BATH, COW, DOG, EGG, FISH, GLASSES, HAT, ICE-CREAM, KANGAROO, LEAF, MIRROR, NUMBER, POPCORN, BLANKET, ROLLER-SKATE, SAND, TOOTHBRUSH, VALENTINE, WASHING-MACHINE

Ernst, Lisa Campbell. *The Turn-Around, Upside-Down Alphabet Book*. New York: Simon & Schuster, 2004.

Readers are invited to see the letters of the alphabet from different perspectives as they turn the book around. A, for example, becomes "a bird's beak, a drippy ice-cream cone, a point of a wishing star" when seen from different angles. This book is an ideal complement to sign language programs because it encourages children to see things in different ways. Signs to use with this story: letters A–Z

Ernst, Lisa Campbell. *Wake Up, It's Spring!* New York: HarperCollins, 2004.

Word spreads to all the animals that spring has arrived, and they celebrate. This simple picture book is great for introducing animal signs and contains a brief text and lots of bright, large illustrations perfect for storytimes. Signs to use with this story: WINTER, SUN, SPRING, WAKE-UP, WORM, SEED, BUG, RABBIT, BIRD, CAT, DOG, BABY, BROTHER, SISTER, MOTHER, FATHER, DANCE

Falwell, Cathryn. *David's Drawings*. New York: Lee and Low, 2001.

David sees a tree on the way to school, and when he arrives he decides to draw it, only to have all of his friends add their own touches. This is a wonderful story for celebrating our differences and discussing the ways in which each person contributes something unique to our world. Signs to use with this story: WINTER, TREE, DRAW, FRIEND, BEAUTIFUL, MINE

Falwell, Cathryn. *Feast for Ten*. New York: Clarion, 1993.

An African American family shops for, cooks, and sits down to eat a meal together. This book combines a story with counting elements and would be great for teaching food and number signs. Signs to use with this story: numbers 1–10, STORE, PUMPKIN, PIE, CHICKEN, TOMATO, POTATO, HELP, CAR/TRUCK, WATCH, COOK, TASTE, CAN, CARROT, CHAIR, SHARE, EAT/FOOD

Falwell, Cathryn. *Nicky and Grandpa*. New York: Clarion, 1991.

Set up in a question and answer format, this book follows baby Nicky through a day with his grandfather. Though the book may be a bit small for sharing with larger groups, its colorful pictures and simple style make it perfect for baby and toddler programs, and it would translate well to a storycard format. Signs to use with this story: WHERE, GRANDFATHER, SHOE, RABBIT, BLANKET, GO, BABY

Falwell, Cathryn. *Nicky's Walk*. New York: Clarion, 1991.

Baby Nicky goes for a walk with his mother and discovers all the red, yellow, and blue things in his world, from red shoes to the yellow bananas he eats for lunch. This book is relatively small, but the illustrations are simple and bright and carry well in story-time. The story would also lend itself well to telling as a flannelboard or prop story. Signs to use with this story: RED, YELLOW, BLUE, WALK, MOTHER, BABY, SHOES, HAT, FLOWER, BIRD, APPLE, BANANA, EAT/FOOD

Fleming, Candace. *Muncha Muncha Muncha*. New York: Atheneum, 2002.

With a surprising structure, a humorous twist, and fantastic illustrations by G. Brian Karas, this is a perfect picture book to share with nearly any age group. Mr. McGreely is determined to keep animals out of his garden, but three wily rabbits evade even his most outlandish attempts. Signs to use with this story: RABBIT, EAT/FOOD

Fleming, Denise. *Mama Cat Has Three Kittens*. New York: Henry Holt, 1998.

Two of Mama Cat's kittens do everything she does, while the third marches to the beat of his own drummer. This gorgeous picture book, with its large illustrations and simple text, is wonderful for toddler and family programs. Signs to use with this story: numbers 1–3, CAT, MOTHER, SLEEP

Florian, Douglas. *A Beach Day*. New York: Greenwillow, 1990.

Childlike illustrations and a terse, rhyming text describe a family's trip to the beach. Florian's books are wonderful for toddler and family programs because they break common experiences down to the bare essentials. Signs to use with this story: SUMMER, CAR/TRUCK, PLAY, KITE, SAND, ICE-CREAM, BIRD, SUNSET, FIREWORKS

Florian, Douglas. *A Summer Day*. New York: Greenwillow, 1988.

A family's trip to the swimming hole is described in brief, rhyming text and large illustrations. Signs to use with this story: SUNRISE, BLUE, WAKE-UP, EAT/FOOD, CAR/TRUCK, SWIM, FISHING, SUNSET, BUG, STAR

Florian, Douglas. *A Winter Day*. New York: Greenwillow, 1987.

A family enjoys a winter's day, from the cold light of morning to the orange sunset. Signs to use with this story: WINTER, COLD, SNOW, EAT/FOOD, HAT, SKATE, WHITE, ORANGE, NIGHT

Fox, Mem. *Time for Bed*. San Diego: Harcourt Brace, 1993.

This simple, classic bedtime story urges all the baby animals to sleep, ending with the little girl in her bed. With a large format, beautiful illustrations, and a simple text, this book is easy enough for baby and toddler programs yet appealing enough for family programs. Signs to use with this story: BED, BABY, MOUSE, CAT, COW, HORSE, FISH, SHEEP, BIRD, BEE, SNAKE, DOG, DEER, GOOD-NIGHT

Freymann, Saxton. *How Are You Peeling? Foods with Moods*. New York: Scholastic, 1999.

With unique illustrations created from various fruits, vegetables, and other foods, this book explores emotions. A wonderful book to share with preschoolers, elementary school students, and families. Signs to use with this story: FEEL, HAPPY, SAD, BORED, SHY, SURPRISED, ANGRY, SORRY, JEALOUS, TIRED

Girnis, Meg. *ABC for You and Me*. Morton Grove, Ill.: Whitman, 2000.

This unique take on the standard alphabet book features striking photos of children with Down syndrome interacting with items representing the various letters. Most notable about this book is the fact that Down syndrome is never mentioned; the children are representative of all children. A wonderful book to share during programs emphasizing our similarities. Signs to use with this story: letters A–Z, APPLE, BALL, CAT, DOG, ELEPHANT, FLOWER, GUITAR, HUG, ICE-CREAM, TOY, KITE, LEAF, MIRROR, NEST, ORANGE, PUZZLE, BLANKET, RABBIT, SAND, UMBRELLA, VACUUM-CLEANER, WAGON, STRING

Glaser, Linda. *It's Fall!* Brookfield, Conn.: Millbrook Press, 2001.

Rhyming text describes the sights, sounds, and scents of autumn. Susan Swan's bold cut-paper illustrations make this book a visual treat. Signs to use with this story: FALL, LEAF, RED, ORANGE, YELLOW, GOLD, BROWN, WIND, BUTTERFLY, BUG, WORM, RACCOON, CHIPMUNK, MOON, OWL, PUMPKIN, TREE

Gliori, Debi. *Flora's Surprise*. New York: Scholastic, 2002.

Flora's family works hard in the garden growing flowers and vegetables, but Flora insists that the brick she is tending in a flowerpot will grow into a house—and sure enough, a spring robin builds its nest there. This story is simple enough to use with young children but humorous enough for older kids and adults—in other words, a perfect book for family programs. Signs to use with this story: RABBIT, FLOWER, LETTUCE, MOTHER, FATHER, SISTER, BROTHER, HOUSE, WINTER, BIRD

Hale, Irina. *How I Found a Friend*. New York: Viking, 1992.

Two young boys become friends when their two teddy bears hit it off. This sweet, simple story of a budding friendship is ideal for preschoolers. Signs to use with this story: BOY, BEAR, HAT, FRIEND, MOTHER

Hall, Zoe. *The Apple Pie Tree*. New York: Scholastic, 1996.

Two girls watch their apple tree with anticipation throughout the year, until they can finally pick apples and make a pie. Signs to use with this story: APPLE, RED, PIE, TREE

Hall, Zoe. *Fall Leaves Fall*. New York: Scholastic, 2000.

Two children enjoy the delights of autumn, especially playing in the falling leaves. This story would work well as a flannelboard or just accompanied by showers of construction paper leaves. For an extension activity, have children identify colors of leaves on a flannelboard and teach the color signs. Signs to use with this story: FALL, LEAF, TREE, GREEN, CHANGE, RED, ORANGE, YELLOW, WIND, BIG, SMALL, RAKE, DRINK, EAT/FOOD, COOKIE

Hall, Zoe. *It's Pumpkin Time!* New York: Scholastic, 1994.

A boy and girl grow a pumpkin patch and follow its progress through the seasons. This book would work well as a flannelboard story, but its large, bright illustrations make it a great read-aloud as is for toddler, preschool, and family programs. Signs to use with this story: SUMMER, HALLOWEEN, PUMPKIN, SUN, WATER, FLOWER, YELLOW, GREEN, SMALL, FALL, ORANGE, BIG, HAPPY

Harley, Bill. *Sitting Down to Eat*. Little Rock, Ark.: August House, 1996.

A young boy is just sitting down to eat when a parade of animals comes into his house and asks to share his food. This funny story, with its repetitive structure and funny ending, is great for introducing animal and counting signs and would work well with preschool, elementary, and family audiences. Signs to use with this story: EAT/FOOD, numbers 1–10, ELEPHANT, TIGER, BEAR, LION, HIPPOPOTAMUS, RHINOC-EROS, WHALE, CROCODILE, CATERPILLAR

Heap, Sue. *What Shall We Play?* Cambridge, Mass.: Candlewick, 2002.

Matt, Lily May, and Martha take turns playing each other's favorite games. This story is not only a terrific simple story about friendship, it also has wonderful colorful illustrations and built-in movement activities as the children act out trees, fairies, and Jell-O. This book is ideal for programs introducing sign language because it encourages children to express themselves through gestures and dramatic movement. Signs to use with this story: PLAY, TREE, CAR/TRUCK, CAT, FRIEND

Hennessy, B. G. *Olympics!* New York: Viking, 1996.

With comic illustrations by Michael Chesworth, this humorous overview of the preparation for and what happens during the Olympics is great for storytime sharing. Signs to use with this story: OLYMPICS, SUMMER, WINTER

Hest, Amy. *In the Rain with Baby Duck.* Cambridge, Mass.: Candlewick, 1995.

Baby Duck does *not* like the rain . . . until Grampa finds an umbrella and boots that are just the right size so she can enjoy splashing through puddles without getting wet feet, a wet face, and mud all over her feathers. This oversized picture book makes great use of repetition and a child's perspective and is terrific for preschool and family programs. Signs to use with this story: DUCK, RAIN, MOTHER, FATHER, GRAND-FATHER, PLAY

Hill, Eric. *Spot Bakes a Cake.* New York: Penguin, 1994.

Spot the puppy and his mother bake a cake for his father's birthday. Use this simple story for introducing party signs, food signs, or family signs. Signs to use with this story: MOTHER, FATHER, BIRTHDAY, CHEESE, STORE, CHOCOLATE, CAKE, EGG, MIX, CLEAN, DRAW, HAPPY, BIRTHDAY, DELICIOUS

Hill, Eric. *Spot Goes to the Farm.* New York: Putnam, 1987.

Spot and his father find the baby animals on the farm. With bright illustrations, a brief text, and a lift-the-flap format, this is a great interactive story for smaller groups. Signs to use with this story: DOG, BABY, COW, HORSE, BIRD, RABBIT, CHICKEN, SHEEP, DUCK, PIG, CAT, MOTHER, FATHER

Hill, Eric. *Spot Visits His Grandparents.* New York: Putnam, 1996.

Spot the puppy has an eventful day visiting with his grandparents. A simple story and big, bright illustrations make this story ideal for baby and toddler storytimes. Consider using a squirt bottle during the part of the story where Spot sprays his grandfather with the hose, and extend the story by using any of the ball activities found in the Having a Ball program plan in chapter 8 of this book. Signs to use with this story: DOG, GRANDMOTHER, GRANDFATHER, MOTHER, BALL

Hines, Anna Grossnickle. *What Can You Do in the Rain?; What Can You Do in the Snow?; What Can You Do in the Sun?; What Can You Do in the Wind?* New York: Greenwillow, 1999.

These board books list the activities you can do in each weather situation and would be easy to adapt as a flannelboard, stick puppet, or prop story if the size is too small for your storytime audience. For older children, consider using all four stories and soliciting suggestions from the audience about other things you can do in the rain, snow, sun, and wind. Signs to use with these stories: RAIN, SNOW, SUN, WIND

Holtz, Lara, ed. *Bathtime*. New York: Dorling Kindersley, 2002.
This larger-sized board book shows photos of real babies in the bath and features a simple text that takes readers from getting ready for bathtime to drying off afterward. Signs to use with this story: WASH, numbers 1–3, DUCK, BOAT, FISH, PLAY, GOOD-BYE

Hort, Lenny. *The Seals on the Bus*. New York: Henry Holt, 2000.
This fun twist on "The Wheels on the Bus" features various animals making different sounds. An enjoyable read-aloud for preschool, elementary, and family programs and a great way to introduce animal signs. Signs to use with this story: BUS, SEAL, TIGER, RABBIT, MONKEY, SNAKE, SHEEP, SKUNK, HELP

Hubbell, Patricia. *Sea, Sand, Me!* New York: HarperCollins, 2001.
A young girl describes all the fun she has at the beach, including building sand castles, splashing in the sea, and making a new friend. Signs to use with this story: CAR/ TRUCK, OCEAN, HAT, DIG, SUN, SAND, BIRD, DANCE, FRIEND, LUNCH, COOKIE, FISH

Inkpen, Mick. *Kipper's A to Z: An Alphabet Adventure*. San Diego: Harcourt, 2000.
This alphabet book is unusual in that it actually contains a story, organized by the alphabet. Kipper and his friend Arnold collect items for each letter. The illustrations are bright, large, and simple, and the story itself is full of humor that will appeal to all ages. (Before the title page, Kipper tells a zebra, "We won't need you till much, much later.") A wonderful read-aloud for family programs. Signs to use with this story: letters A–Z, BUG, BOX, BEE, CATERPILLAR, DUCK, ELEPHANT, FROG, GRASSHOP-PER, HAPPY, JUICE, DIRT, NO, ON, PINK, QUIET, RAIN, RAINBOW, TOY, UMBRELLA, WORM, YES

Inkpen, Mick. *Kipper's Lost Ball*. San Diego: Red Wagon Books, 2002.
Kipper the dog has lost his ball. Readers are invited to help him find it as he searches behind several large flaps. The colorful illustrations and excellent use of white back-grounds make this book perfect for interactive storytimes with babies and toddlers. Signs to use with this story: RED, BALL, WHERE, THANK-YOU, PLAY, GOOD-BYE

Inkpen, Mick. *Kipper's Rainy Day*. San Diego: Harcourt, 1991.
Kipper the dog goes for a walk in the rain and meets other animals who love the rain. Large, bright illustrations and an interactive lift-the-flap format make this story ideal for toddler and family programs. Signs to use with this story: DOG, RAIN, UMBRELLA, FROG, SHEEP, PIG, CAT, SUN

Inkpen, Mick. *Kipper's Snowy Day*. San Diego: Harcourt, 1996.
Kipper and his friend Tiger play in the snow. This book is slightly longer than most in the *Kipper* series and so would best be used in preschool storytimes. Signs to use with this story: DOG, SNOW

Inkpen, Mick. *Kipper's Sunny Day*. San Diego: Harcourt, 1991.

Kipper and his friend Tiger spend a sunny day at the beach. With a brief and interactive text, large lift-the-flap format, and winsome illustrations, this book is great for toddler, preschool, and family programs. Signs to use with this story: DOG, SUN, UMBRELLA, EAT/FOOD, BALL, ICE CREAM, GOOD-BYE

Johnson, Stephen T. *Alphabet City*. New York: Viking, 1995.

With startlingly realistic-looking paintings, Johnson explores objects in the city that seem to bear letter shapes. A traffic light seen from the side becomes an *E*, and the twin arches of a bridge form an M. This is a wonderful way to introduce the manual alphabet while encouraging youngsters to see things from a new perspective. Signs to use with this story: letters A–Z

Johnson, Stephen T. *City by Numbers*. New York: Viking, 1998.

Johnson's imaginative picture book features paintings of objects throughout a city, and readers must find the numbers hidden there—a 3, for example, in the curlicue of a wrought-iron gate, or the way two tall towers seem to form an 11. This is a wonderful visual activity to accompany programs introducing ASL numbers or any program focusing on sign language. Signs to use with this story: numbers 1–21

Jonas, Ann. *Splash!* New York: Greenwillow, 1995.

A child describes her backyard pond and invites readers to count the animals in it on each spread. This is a great book for using numbers with preschoolers and older children because it goes beyond basic counting. It could also be used to teach animal signs. Signs to use with this story: TURTLE, FROG, FISH, DOG, CAT, BUG, BIRD, GIRL, numbers 1–12

Keats, Ezra Jack. *The Snowy Day*. New York: Viking, 1962.

Peter spends a day playing in the snow in this classic story. Signs to use with this story: SNOW, WALK, SNOWMAN, MOTHER, BATH, MELT, SLEEP, SUN

Keller, Holly. *Farfellina and Marcel*. New York: Greenwillow, 2002.

Marcel the goose is worried when his friend Farfellina the caterpillar disappears for a very long time . . . only to be delighted when she emerges from her cocoon as a butterfly and the two can fly through the sky together. Signs to use with this story: BIRD, CATERPILLAR, BUTTERFLY, FRIEND

Kennedy, X. J. *Elympics*. New York: Philomel, 1999.

These humorous poems, divided into sections for the Summer and Winter Olympics, imagine elephants competing in the various events and are accompanied by hysterical illustrations of the competitive pachyderms. Signs to use with this story: ELEPHANT, OLYMPICS, BICYCLE, SWIM, VOLLEYBALL, GYMNASTICS, DIVE, THROW, SUMMER, WINTER, SKATE, SKI, WIN, GOLD

Kutner, Merrily. *Down on the Farm*. New York: Holiday House, 2004.

All sorts of things happen down on the farm, from the rooster crowing to the crows cawing to the dog climbing onto the roof! Wil Hillenbrand's colorful illustrations combine with Kutner's rhythmic text for a great storytime read-aloud. Signs to use with this story: FARM, ROOSTER, GOAT, BIRD, HORSE, COW, DUCK, TURKEY, DOG, PIG, CAT, QUIET

Lawrence, Michael. *Baby Loves*. New York: Dorling Kindersley, 1999.

Baby loves many things, but mommy and daddy don't love anything more than they love baby. With large, colorful illustrations, this book is great for baby and toddler programs, and the repetitive format makes it easy to cut out parts of the story should you need to shorten it. Signs to use with this story: MOTHER, FATHER, EAT/FOOD, BEAR, CAT, SHOES, FLOWER, GRANDMOTHER, HAT, SUN, RAIN, DRUM, DUCK, BATH, BED, BABY, LOVE

Lawrence, Michael. *Baby Loves Hugs and Kisses*. New York: Dorling Kindersley, 2000.

Baby loves hugs and kisses from each and every member of the family, but sleepytime hugs and kisses are the best. With large, colorful illustrations, this is a great storytime book, and, as an added bonus, the repetitive structure makes it easy to cut the story short if you have a restless group. Signs to use with this story: BABY, MOTHER, FATHER, GRANDMOTHER, GRANDFATHER, BED, KISS

LeSeig, Theo. *Ten Apples up on Top!* New York: Random House, 1961.

This classic beginning reader makes a great read-aloud and a fun, if complex, flannelboard. A wonderful way to introduce number signs for preschool and elementary children. Signs to use with this story: numbers 1–10, APPLE, LION, TIGER, DOG, BEAR, UMBRELLA

Lindgren, Barbro. *Sam's Ball*. New York: Morrow Junior Books, 1982.

Sam wants to play with his ball, but kitty has other ideas. This simple story is great for little ones, but the small size of the book and illustrations mean that it's best adapted as a prop or flannelboard story. Signs to use with this story: BALL, PLAY, CAT

Liu, Jae Soo. *Yellow Umbrella*. La Jolla, Calif.: Kane-Miller, 2002.

This wordless picture book gives aerial views of a city on a gray, rainy day, when the only spots of color are umbrellas. The book also includes the words and music to an original song titled "Underneath the Sky," which could be used to supplement the story. Have children identify the colors and count the umbrellas in the pictures. Signs to use with this story: YELLOW, BLUE, RED, GREEN, ORANGE, PINK, PURPLE, numbers 1–10

London, Jonathan. *Froggy Goes to School*. New York: Puffin, 1996.

Irrepressible Froggy has fun on the first day of school, even though his antics come close to getting him in trouble. With its outlandish sound effects and upbeat title character, this is a great story for sharing with preschool and elementary audiences. Signs to use with this story: FROG, SCHOOL, BUS, DESK, PAY-ATTENTION

Luciani, Brigitte. *How Will We Get to the Beach? A Guessing-Game Story*. New York: North-South Books, 2000.

Roxanne wants to go to the beach but has difficulties fitting her turtle, her book, her ball, her umbrella, and, of course, her baby, into the various means of transportation she tries. Readers are invited to figure out what won't fit each time, making this story instantly interactive. Perfect for preschool and family audiences. Signs to use with this story: MOTHER, BABY, BALL, BOOK, TURTLE, UMBRELLA, CAR/TRUCK, BUS, BICYCLE, SKATEBOARD, BOAT, BALLOON, HORSE

Marshall, Janet Perry. *My Camera at the Zoo*. Boston: Little, Brown, 1989.

Readers see zoo animals through the lens of a child's camera and must guess the identity of each animal based on seeing a part of it. With bold, colorful illustrations and a great premise, this interactive book is perfect for toddler, preschool, and family programs. Signs to use with this story: CAMERA, Z-O-O (spelled), BEAR, CROCODILE, SNAKE, MONKEY, LEOPARD, BIRD

Martin, Bill, Jr. *Brown Bear, Brown Bear, What Do You See?* New York: Henry Holt, 1967. Eric Carle's classic illustrations make this the consummate color book. The illustrations are large enough to share with a large group, or this book can be easily adapted to a flannelboard or stick puppet story. The story could be used to introduce color signs, animal signs, or both. Signs to use with this story: BROWN, RED, YELLOW, BLUE, GREEN, PURPLE, WHITE, BLACK, GOLD, BEAR, BIRD, DUCK, HORSE, FROG, CAT, DOG, SHEEP, FISH

Martin, Bill, Jr. *Chicka Chicka Boom Boom.* New York: Simon & Schuster, 1989. With a rhythmic, rhyming text; lots of humor; and clear, bright illustrations by Lois Ehlert, this book is justifiably a storytime favorite. Add a new dimension to this classic tale by using manual letters during the story. This book also works very well as a flannelboard. Signs to use with this story: letters A–Z, TREE, SUN, MOON

McDonnell, Flora. *I Love Animals.* Cambridge, Mass.: Candlewick Press, 1994. McDonnell's oversized, bold and bright picture books are perfect for storytime, and this book is no exception. With a brief text, the book is ideal for babies and toddlers. Invite children to act out the animals while you read the text, then share the signs. Signs to use with this story: DOG, DUCK, CHICKEN, GOAT, DONKEY, COW, PIG, HORSE, SHEEP, CAT, TURKEY, LOVE

McDonnell, Flora. *Splash!* Cambridge, Mass.: Candlewick, 1999. McDonnell's oversized, bold illustrations are perfect for storytime sharing, and the simple text is ideal for baby, toddler, and family programs. Use this story to teach simple animal signs, and extend it by squirting water when the baby elephant in the story does. Signs to use with this story: HOT, ELEPHANT, TIGER, RHINOCEROS, BABY, WATER, HAPPY

McMillan, Bruce. *Mouse Views: What the Class Pet Saw.* New York: Holiday House, 1993. This wonderfully unique book is perfect for sharing with preschoolers or elementary audiences. Readers are invited to explore a school from the point of view of an escaped pet mouse, and each page offers a unique perspective on an everyday object, whose identity readers must try to figure out. This is an excellent discussion starter for the importance of using our eyes in American Sign Language. For a fun extension of this book, use a digital camera to create your own "mouse views" of objects in your storytime area, and invite kids to guess what they are, or let kids take turns helping you find objects to take close-ups of. Signs to use with this story: MOUSE, SCHOOL, BALL, BOOK, CHALK (WRITE)

Merriam, Eve. *Ten Rosy Roses.* New York: HarperCollins, 1999. Ten students take turns picking roses for their teacher. This counting book features large, bright illustrations and a repetitive rhyming structure that's perfect for toddler and family storytimes. Signs to use with this story: FLOWER, numbers 1–10, BEE, TREE

Milich, Zoran. *The City ABC Book*. Tonawonda, N.Y.: Kids Can Press, 2001.

Readers are invited to find the letters of the alphabet hidden in city architecture in this inventive picture book. The letters are highlighted in red in the black and white photos, encouraging children to use their eyes in new ways and see things from a new perspective. Signs to use with this story: letters A–Z, CITY

Miller, Margaret. *I Love Colors*. New York: Little Simon, 1999.

This colorful board book features a super-simple text and close-up photos of babies sporting different colored items. Signs to use with this story: RED, PURPLE, ORANGE, BLUE, GREEN, BABY

Miller, Virginia. *Ten Red Apples*. Cambridge, Mass.: Candlewick, 2002.

Bartholomew Bear loves many things about his apple tree, but the best part is picking the apples and making pie. This wonderful counting book has oversized pictures just right for sharing in toddler and family storytimes. Signs to use with this story: BEAR, APPLE, TREE, RAIN, CAT, EAT/FOOD, numbers 1–10

Minarik, Else Holmelund. *It's Spring!* New York: Greenwillow, 1989.

Two little cats, giddy in the spring, make silly boasts about what they could jump over but decide it's more fun just to jump over each other. This repetitive story is great for toddler and family programs and could be presented as a straight read-aloud or a prop story with two stuffed cats. Signs to use with this story: SPRING, CAT, HAPPY, FLOWER, TREE, HOUSE, ISLAND, MOUNTAIN, MOON, SUN, YOU

Minarik, Else Holmelund. *Little Bear's Valentine*. New York: HarperCollins, 2003.

This picture book, featuring Little Bear of the classic *I Can Read* series, takes Little Bear on a journey to find out who his secret admirer is. Children will love picking out the clues in the pictures as Mother Bear follows him on his journey. This sweet story with a satisfying ending is wonderful for programs for toddlers, preschoolers, and families. Signs to use with this story: BEAR, VALENTINE, MOTHER, GIRL, CHICKEN, DUCK, OWL, SURPRISE, PARTY, KISS

Mockford, Caroline. *Cleo in the Snow*. Cambridge, Mass.: Barefoot Books, 2002.

Cleo the cat and Jasper the dog have an eventful sleigh ride, but they prefer being inside and warm. Large, bright illustrations and a very simple text make this story perfect for toddler or family programs. Signs to use with this story: CAT, DOG, SNOW

Modell, Frank. *One Zillion Valentines*. New York: Greenwillow, 1981.

Marvin and Milton want to send valentines to everyone they know, so they decide to make handmade cards. This story lends itself well to extension activities such as match-the-heart games and make-your-own-valentine crafts. Signs to use with this story: VALENTINE, DRAW, RED, WHITE, SURPRISE, CANDY, HAPPY, DAY

Murphy, Mary. *I Kissed the Baby!* Cambridge, Mass.: Candlewick, 2003.

With dynamic black-and-white graphics tinged with splashes of color, this book's simple text features various barnyard animals sharing their excitement over the new baby on the farm. Wonderful for baby and toddler programs or to introduce farm animal signs to older children. Signs to use with this story: BABY, FISH, BIRD, SQUIRREL, BUG, FROG, BUTTERFLY, MOUSE, DUCK, KISS

Newcome, Zita. *Toddlerobics: Animal Fun*. Cambridge, Mass.: Candlewick, 1999.

A group of wiggly toddlers go to exercise class, where they act out different animals. Teach the signs for the animals as you read the book, then invite children to act out each animal like the children in the book. Signs to use with this story: PENGUIN, FISH, CRAB, DUCK, FROG, LION, KANGAROO, MONKEY, ELEPHANT, SNAKE, HORSE, BUTTERFLY, WORM

Numeroff, Laura. *If You Give a Mouse a Cookie*. New York: HarperCollins, 1985.

"If you give a mouse a cookie . . ." Well, we all know where that leads. Use this book to teach food signs for preschool, elementary, and family audiences. Signs to use with this story: MOUSE, COOKIE, MILK, STRAW, NAPKIN, MIRROR, SWEEP, WASH, SLEEP, BOOK, DRAW, NAME, PEN, TAPE

Numeroff, Laura. *If You Take a Mouse to School*. New York: HarperCollins, 2002.

In this cause-and-effect take on the school day, the famous mouse works his magic once more. With enough humor for older children and family programs, this book is a great way to introduce signs for the many things that happen at school. Though the illustrations are a bit small for sharing with large groups, this book would work well as a flannelboard or prop story. Signs to use with this story: MOUSE, SCHOOL, LUNCH, SANDWICH, BACKPACK, MATH, SCIENCE, BATHROOM, BOOK, WRITE, READ, SOCCER, BASKETBALL, SKATEBOARD

Oxenbury, Helen. *Family*. New York: Simon & Schuster, 1981.

This simple board book introduces the various members of the family. Though it is a bit small for sharing with larger groups, this book would translate well to a storycard or stick puppet format. Signs to use with this story: FAMILY, MOTHER, FATHER, SISTER, BROTHER, GRANDMOTHER, GRANDFATHER, BABY

Oxenbury, Helen. *It's My Birthday*. Cambridge, Mass.: Candlewick, 1993.

A young child asks the animals for help with every part of making a birthday cake, but especially with eating it. Though the illustrations in this simple picture book are a bit small for sharing with larger groups, it would adapt well to telling as a flannelboard or prop story. Signs to use with this story: BIRTHDAY, CAKE, CHICKEN, EGG, BEAR, BUTTER, MILK, CAT, SALT, PIG, SUGAR, DOG, CHERRY, MONKEY, EAT/FOOD

Oxenbury, Helen. *Say Goodnight*. New York: Little Simon, 1987.

Helen Oxenbury's bright, large-format board books are ideal for baby storytimes, and this is no exception. Three babies play until they are worn out and then fall asleep. Encourage parents to imitate the actions in the text, swinging babies up high and down low, as you read. Signs to use with this story: BABY, GOOD-NIGHT

Poulsson, Emilie. *Baby's Breakfast*. New York: Henry Holt, 1996.

The cow, chicken, bee, and baker all work together to make sure baby gets breakfast. With colorful illustrations, a unique lift-the-flap style, and a great concept, this book is justifiably a storytime classic. Unfortunately its small size makes it difficult to use with larger groups. It adapts well to telling as a flannelboard, however. Signs to use with this story: BABY, EAT/FOOD, COW, MILK, CHICKEN, EGG, BEE, HONEY, BREAD, THANK-YOU

Powell, Richard. *I Spy in the Garden*. New York: Puffin, 1993.

With colorful illustrations against a white background, this interactive book invites readers to guess what's behind each flap. Signs to use with this story: RABBIT, WORM, BUTTERFLY, CAT, FISH, BUG, CATERPILLAR, DOG

Poydar, Nancy. *Snip, Snip . . . Snow!* New York: Holiday House, 1997.

Sophie yearns for snow . . . but when none comes, she and her classmates decide to make paper snowflakes of their own. This school story is great for preschool and elementary audiences and lends itself to extension activities involving making snowflakes. Signs to use with this story: WINTER, SNOW, CUT, NONE, PLAY

Rice, Eve. *Sam Who Never Forgets.* New York: Greenwillow, 1977.

Sam the zookeeper never, ever forgets to feed the animals. This simple story is a wonderful way to introduce animal signs and is simple enough for toddler and preschool programs. Though the book is on the small side for sharing with large groups, it would adapt well as a flannelboard or prop story. Signs to use with this story: FORGET, GIRAFFE, THANK-YOU, MONKEY, BEAR, CROCODILE, LION, ELEPHANT

Rockwell, Anne. *Apples and Pumpkins.* New York: Macmillan, 1989.

This classic story, with its simple text and illustrations, is a standard for fall programs. Spice it up by using signs. Signs to use with this story: APPLE, PUMPKIN, CHICKEN, TURKEY, TREE, HALLOWEEN

Rockwell, Anne. *Growing Like Me.* San Diego: Harcourt, 2001.

This nonfiction picture book describes the many things that grow and what they will become. Perfect for preschoolers. Signs to use with this story: FLOWER, BERRY, EGG, BIRD, CATERPILLAR, BUTTERFLY, POLLYWOG, FROG, BABY, DUCK, FISH, NUT, TREE, BOY, ME

Rockwell, Anne. *Mr. Panda's Painting.* New York: Macmillan, 1993.

Mr. Panda goes to the art store to buy some more paint and is delighted to find items that match the colors of his paint as he walks home. This story is an ideal way to introduce color signs for preschool and family groups. As a story extender, have children vote on their favorite colors and show the tally on a flipchart or flannelboard. Signs to use with this story: RED, BLUE, YELLOW, ORANGE, GREEN, PURPLE

Rockwell, Anne. *My Spring Robin.* New York: Macmillan, 1989.

A little girl waits impatiently for her favorite robin to come back in the spring, experiencing all the other joys of spring while she waits. Signs to use with this story: BIRD, SUMMER, FALL, SPRING, BEE, FLOWER, TREE, RAIN, CAT, SING

Rockwell, Anne. *Two Blue Jays.* New York: Walker, 2003.

A little girl describes the spring that two blue jays made their nest outside her classroom and she and her classmates studied them and their babies. This wonderful book for preschoolers and elementary students incorporates a great deal of factual information in the text. Signs to use with this story: SPRING, BLUE, BIRD, numbers 1–2, LOOK-FOR, EAT/FOOD, EGG, BABY

Rockwell, Anne. *Valentine's Day.* New York: HarperCollins, 2001.

A class makes valentines for their friend in Japan, listing all the reasons they miss her. Signs to use with this story: VALENTINE, SCHOOL, FRIEND, PLAY, I-LOVE-YOU

Rockwell, Anne, and Harlow Rockwell. *The First Snowfall.* New York: Macmillan, 1987.

A little girl describes a day in the snow. This simple picture book is ideal for baby and toddler programs, as well as sharing with family groups. Signs to use with this story: SNOW, MITTENS, HAT, SHOES, JACKET, PANTS, SNOWMAN, CAR/TRUCK, SLED, SKI, PLAY, HOT, CHOCOLATE

Roddie, Shen. *Too Close Friends.* New York: Dial, 1997.

Hippo and Pig are best friends . . . until trimming the hedge between their houses leads to a little *too* much knowledge of each other. Preschoolers and older kids will delight at the humorous misunderstanding between the two friends and their antics when neither knows the other is watching. (Hippo, for example, tends to chew on his toenails.) Signs to use with this story: PIG, HIPPOPOTAMUS, FRIEND, days of the week

Rogers, Paul. *What Will the Weather Be Like Today?* New York: Scholastic, 1989.

With bright, simple illustrations and a brief text, this story offers many possible answers to the titular question. Signs to use with this story: BIRD, WIND, HOT, SNOW, COLD, RAIN, FROG, BEE, DUCK, FISH, SUN, PLAY, RAINBOW

Rylant, Cynthia. *Henry and Mudge in the Green Time.* New York: Simon & Schuster, 1987.

With their strong focus on simple stories with a definite beginning, middle, and end, beginning readers are often easy to adapt for storytime use. The *Henry and Mudge* series contains many stories that are short and simple, perfect for telling aloud using props in programs. "The Bath" from this collection is a great example. Make stick puppets of Henry and Mudge (or use stuffed animals) and use a squirt bottle to spray your audience when Mudge tries to dry off from his bath. Signs to use with this story: BATH, DOG, WATER

Serfozo, Mary. *Plumply, Dumply Pumpkin.* New York: Simon & Schuster, 2001.

A little tiger goes on a quest to find the perfect pumpkin, from which to make the perfect jack-o'-lantern. Serfozo's silly text and Valeria Petrone's bright, whimsical illustrations make this a fun read-aloud for toddler and family programs. Signs to use with this story: PUMPKIN, TIGER, FATHER

Serfozo, Mary. *Who Said Red?* New York: Macmillan, 1988.

This playful picture book is great for introducing color signs and is also available in a big-book format. Signs to use with this story: RED, GREEN, BLUE, YELLOW, PURPLE, PINK, ORANGE, BLACK, WHITE

Sheppard, Jeff. *Splish, Splash.* New York: Macmillan, 1994.

A series of animals splash into the water, each making a unique sound. This story would work well as a read-aloud, a flannelboard, or a prop story told with stuffed animals. Signs to use with this story: BEE, MOUSE, PIG, DOG, COW, DUCK, CAT, FROG

Simmons, Jane. *Come Along, Daisy!* Boston: Little, Brown, 1997.

Daisy the duckling has so much fun playing at the pond that she forgets to stay close to her mother. This book, with its large illustrations and simple text, is perfect for baby and toddler storytimes. Signs to use with this story: DUCK, MOTHER, FISH, BUG, FROG, BUTTERFLY

Simmons, Jane. *Daisy's Day Out.* New York: Little, Brown, 2000.

Daisy the duckling and her mother go to see Granny, a trip that takes them up the slippery bank, under the willow, through the long grass, and finally into the pool. This large board book for the youngest storytimers is well suited to gestures and audience participation to enact Daisy's movements. Signs to use with this story: DUCK, GRANDMOTHER

Slobodkina, Esphyr. *Caps for Sale*. New York: Harper and Row, 1940.

The tale of the peddler and the monkeys who steal his caps is a storytime classic, and it's also a great way to introduce color signs. Whether you read the book aloud, tell the story using a flannelboard or other props, or just tell the story straight out, the participation aspect of the tale, combined with learning the signs, will draw in storytime participants from toddlers to teenagers. Signs to use with this story: HAT, GRAY, BROWN, BLUE, RED, TREE, SLEEP, MONKEY

Spafford, Suzy. *Fall Is for Friends*. New York: Scholastic, 2003.

Suzy Ducken and her friend Emily are impatient for the leaves to fall, so they devise ways to encourage the leaves to leave their branches. This cute story lends itself well to audience participation and would make a great flannelboard story. Signs to use with this story: FALL, LEAF, FRIEND, CUT, DANCE, SING, WIND

Spanyol, Jessica. *Carlo Likes Colors*. Cambridge, Mass.: Candlewick, 2003.

Carlo the giraffe explores the many colors in his town, from the yellow in the fields to the pink ice cream he eats on his way home. Large, charming illustrations and a brief text make this book great for younger listeners. Signs to use with this story: GIRAFFE, YELLOW, RED, BLACK, BROWN, GREEN, WHITE, PURPLE, ORANGE, BLUE, PINK

Spanyol, Jessica. *Carlo Likes Counting*. Cambridge, Mass.: Candlewick, 2002.

In this large-format, bright and bold story, Carlo the giraffe takes a trip through his town, counting objects one to ten. Signs to use with this story: numbers 1–10, GIRAFFE

Spinelli, Eileen. *I Know It's Autumn*. New York: HarperCollins, 2004.

A young girl lists the many ways she knows autumn has arrived, from the late morning light to the hayride and campfire she shares with her family. Signs to use with this story: FALL, PUMPKIN, JACKET, BUS, LEAF, RED, GOLD, BROWN, TURKEY, APPLE, FIRE

Steig, William. *Pete's a Pizza*. New York: HarperCollins, 1998.

Pete's in a bad mood, which means it's time for his parents to cheer him up by pretending to knead him, toss him, and garnish him like a pizza. This silly parent-and-child game is great for food programs or any programs that focus on the sillier side of life. Signs to use with this story: PIZZA, TOMATO, CHEESE, COOK

Stoeke, Janet Morgan. *Minerva Louise at School*. New York: Dutton, 1996.

Like Bruce McMillan's *Mouse Views: What the Class Pet Saw*, this is a marvelous book for launching discussions of visual perception, a topic intimately tied to ASL. Minerva Louise the chicken goes to school, where she misinterprets everything she sees. Signs to use with this story: CHICKEN, SCHOOL, FLAG, CHAIR, TRASH-CAN

Stoeke, Janet Morgan. *Rainy Day*. New York: Dutton, 1999.

This board book, starring Minerva Louise the chicken, is too small for storytime sharing, but don't let that stop you from using this great story. After attempting to take refuge from the rain under a lamb, Minerva Louise decides she might as well embrace getting wet. With only two characters, this story would easily translate to a flannelboard or stick puppet format or could be told using stuffed animals. Use a squirt bottle to spray your audience when Minerva Louise splashes into the water. Signs to use with this story: CHICKEN, LAMB, RAIN, BATH

Szekeres, Cyndy. *Toby Counts His Marbles.* New York: Little Simon, 2000.
Toby wants to play with his marbles, but there's only one in the box. As he finds them and puts them in the box, he counts them. This book is a bit small for storytimes but would work well as a simple flannelboard with marbles to count. In addition, by making the marbles different colors, this story could be used to introduce color signs as well as number signs. Signs to use with this story: numbers 1–10, MOUSE, PLAY, LOOK-FOR, color signs

Tafuri, Nancy. *The Ball Bounced.* New York: Greenwillow, 1989.
This book follows the simple chain of events set off when baby's ball bounces through the house. Though the size of this book is relatively small, the pictures are large and colorful. Signs to use with this story: BALL, CAT, FISH, DOG, BIRD, BABY

Tafuri, Nancy. *This Is the Farmer.* New York: Greenwillow, 1994.
A simple chain of events follows the farmer from his house, where he gets ready to do his morning chores, to the barn where he milks the cow. Tafuri's trademark oversized illustrations and clean, simple text make this book perfect for baby and toddler audiences. Signs to use with this story: FARM, KISS, DOG, BUG, CAT, MOUSE, DONKEY, COW

Tafuri, Nancy. *Where Did Bunny Go?* New York: Scholastic, 2001.
Bunny and Bird are best friends. In this simple story, appropriate for toddlers and up, they play hide and seek with their friends in the snow, and Bird briefly thinks Bunny does not want to be friends any longer, until Bunny sets her straight. A large format, gorgeous illustrations, and a simple story make this a natural choice for group reading. Signs to use with this story: BIRD, RABBIT, TREE, FRIEND, SNOW, PLAY, SQUIRREL/CHIPMUNK, HAPPY

Thompson, Lauren. *Little Quack.* New York: Simon & Schuster, 2003.
Little Quack's four brothers and sisters take the plunge into the pond, one by one, until Little Quack is the only one left on shore. With large and bright illustrations, a bouncy text, and a unique "quack-u-lator" at the bottom of the page that helps count the ducklings as they dive in, this is a fun picture book for toddlers and preschoolers. For an extra-fun touch, use a squirt bottle each time one of the ducklings splashes into the pond. Signs to use with this story: DUCK, MOTHER, numbers 1–5

Thompson, Lauren. *Mouse's First Summer.* New York: Simon & Schuster, 2004.
Mouse and Minka tag along on a picnic and experience the joys of summer, from tasty watermelons to fireworks. Simple text and colorful illustrations make this book ideal for toddler and family programs. It's also good for introducing color signs. Signs to use with this story: SUMMER, MOUSE, PLAY, WATERMELON, BUG, KITE, DRINK, BREAD, PEANUT-BUTTER, JELLY, EAT/FOOD, FIREWORKS, HOORAY, RED, BLACK, GREEN, BLUE, ORANGE, YELLOW, WHITE, BROWN, PURPLE

Van Laan, Nancy. *Tickle Tum!* New York: Atheneum, 2001.
A mother rabbit keeps her little one entertained during dinner. This book is terrific for baby storytimes, with its bouncy rhyming text and large, colorful illustrations. Signs to use with this story: MOTHER, BABY, EAT/FOOD, BED, I-LOVE-YOU

Van Rynbach, Iris. *Five Little Pumpkins.* Honesdale, Pa.: Boyds Mill Press, 1995.
This illustrated version of the classic rhyme features Halloween scenes and trick-or-treaters, as well as a countdown of pumpkins. Signs to use with this story: numbers 1–5, PUMPKIN, WITCHES, FUN, WIND

Wallace, Nancy Elizabeth. *Apples, Apples, Apples.* New York: Winslow Press, 2000.
The Rabbit family visits an apple orchard, where they pick apples and learn about the different kinds of apples. The book also includes a recipe for applesauce and directions for a craft. Signs to use with this story: APPLE, RED, YELLOW, GREEN, TREE

Walsh, Ellen Stoll. *Mouse Count.* San Diego: Harcourt Brace, 1991.
Ten mice are so busy playing that they forget to watch for snakes . . . but when one finds them and puts them in his jar to eat, they cleverly trick him and escape. This story is easy enough to use with toddlers yet clever enough to amuse older children. This book adapts especially well as a prop story, using toy mice, a jar, a rock, and a toy snake. Signs to use with this story: numbers 1–10, MOUSE, SNAKE, EAT/FOOD

Walsh, Ellen Stoll. *Mouse Paint.* San Diego: Harcourt Brace, 1989.
Three white mice discover jars of red, yellow, and blue paint and all the other colors they can make. This book serves a wide range of ages, from toddlers just learning colors to older children who are familiar with the color wheel. The book itself is large enough for sharing, but the story would also work well with props such as paint to mix on an overhead projector screen. Signs to use with this story: MOUSE, CAT, number 3, WHITE, RED, YELLOW, BLUE, ORANGE, GREEN, PURPLE

Walton, Rick. *Bunny Day: Telling Time from Breakfast to Bedtime.* New York: HarperCollins, 2002.
A family of bunnies spends the day together working in the garden, having a picnic lunch, and playing. This is a wonderful book for introducing family signs or time signs for preschool, elementary, or family audiences. Signs to use with this story: RABBIT, FAMILY, FATHER, MOTHER, MORNING, BREAKFAST, PLAY, LUNCH, SLEEP, HUNGRY, DINNER, BOOK, GOOD, NIGHT, time signs

Walton, Rick. *My Two Hands, My Two Feet.* New York: Putnam, 2000.
This book actually contains two separate stories—read one way, it's about hands, but turn it over and the story is about feet. The hand story invites children to show the things they can do with their hands and would be a great hand warm-up or lead-in to discussions of sign language. Either story would work well with programs about body parts. Signs to use in this story: HAND, BUTTERFLY, FRIEND, HAPPY

Wellington, Monica. *Apple Farmer Annie.* New York: Dutton, 2001.
Apple Farmer Annie picks her apples in the fall; sorts them and makes cider, applesauce, and other goodies; then drives into the city to sell them. Large, engaging illustrations and brief text make this book ideal for toddler and family programs. The story lends itself especially well to extension activities about colors and sorting. Signs to use with this story: APPLE, TREE, RED, YELLOW, GREEN, COOK, SELL, CITY, BUY

Wellington, Monica. *Bunny's First Snowflake*. New York: Dutton, 2000.

Bunny and his friends get ready for winter, just in time for the first flake of snow. With a larger size and simple, colorful illustrations, this board book would work in programs for just about any age. It would also make a great flannelboard. Signs to use with this story: WINTER, RABBIT, WIND, SQUIRREL, BEAR, RACCOON, MOUSE, SKUNK, SNOW, SLEEP

Wells, Rosemary. *Bunny Cakes*. New York: Viking, 1997.

Max wants to make an earthworm cake for his grandmother's birthday but has some difficulty explaining to the man at the grocery store what he needs. Max circumvents his inability to write by drawing pictures, but this story is a great jumping off point for discussions with preschoolers and older children about the importance and challenges of communication. Signs to use with this story: RABBIT, BIRTHDAY, GRAND-MOTHER, CAKE, EGG, MILK, STAR, HEART, FLOWER, HAPPY

Wells, Rosemary. *Bunny Party*. New York: Viking, 2001.

Ruby decides to hold a special party for Grandma's birthday, and Max decides to invite some guests of his own. This adventure of bossy older sister Ruby and spirited little brother Max is a funny read-aloud for preschool and family programs that also incorporates counting to ten. Signs to use with this story: RABBIT, GRANDMOTHER, BIRTHDAY, PARTY, numbers 1–10, ICE-CREAM, CANDY

Wells, Rosemary. *Max's Bath*. New York: Dial, 1985.

Big sister Ruby does everything she can to get little Max to take a bath, only to wind up needing one herself. With colorful, charming illustrations and a simple text, this story is perfect for babies and toddlers; however, because of the relatively small size of the book, it may work best in storytime as a storycard or flannelboard story. Signs to use with this story: DIRTY, WASH, RABBIT

Williams, Laura Ellen. *ABC Kids*. New York: Philomel, 2000.

Large, crisp photos of real kids distinguish this alphabet book, which is perfect for storytime sharing. Each letter features an object or action as well. Signs to use with this story: letters A–Z, KID, APPLE, BATH, CLOWN, DIRT, ELEPHANT, GUINEA-PIG, HOT-DOG, ICE-CREAM, CANDY, KISS, LAUGH, MASK, SLEEP, ORANGE, POPCORN, QUEEN, FLOWER, SPOON, VEGETABLE, WATER-MELON, YO-YO, ZIPPER

Williams, Sue. *Dinnertime!* San Diego: Harcourt, 2001.

This wonderfully clever picture book is great for toddler, preschool, or family programs. A fox keeps chasing five little rabbits, sneaking up on them and shouting, "Dinnertime!" One by one the rabbits disappear; astute children will notice them tumbling out of sight into holes in the ground, not being eaten as the text suggests. Finally, we see all the rabbits at home with Mom, and we understand that fox has only been calling them home to dinner, not announcing his intentions. Signs to use with this story: RABBIT, FOX, numbers 1–5, EAT/FOOD, DINNER, TIME, MOTHER

Williams, Sue. *I Went Walking*. San Diego: Harcourt, 1990.

Perfect for baby and toddler audiences, Williams's simple rhyming story features a young child taking a walk and running into different animals. This story lends itself especially well to telling with stick puppets or a flannelboard. Signs to use with this story: WALK, BLACK, BROWN, RED, GREEN, PINK, YELLOW, CAT, HORSE, COW, DUCK, PIG, DOG

Wilson, Karma. *Bear Wants More.* New York: Simon & Schuster, 2003.

Bear wakes up from his winter sleep hungry as can be, and no matter how much he eats, he always wants *more.* Whether by design or by chance, the cover illustration of this book appears as if the animals are signing MORE, and the story is a fun read-aloud for all ages, as well as a great way to introduce animal signs. Signs to use with this story: BEAR, MORE, EAT/FOOD, MOUSE, RABBIT, BIRD, PARTY, SURPRISE, STUCK, SLEEP

Ziefert, Harriet. *I Swapped My Dog.* Boston: Houghton Mifflin, 1998.

A farmer makes a series of trades for various animals, only to find that what he really wants is the dog he swapped away in the first place. This humorous story with large, bright illustrations is a great way to introduce animal signs and is both brief enough for toddler programs and humorous enough to share with older kids. Signs to use with this story: DOG, HORSE, DONKEY/MULE, GOAT, SHEEP, COW, PIG, CHICKEN, CAT, FRIEND

Ziefert, Harriet. *My Funny Valentine.* New York: Puffin, 2002.

A valentine narrates his progress through the mail in this charming lift-the-flap book. With a simple storyline and not too much text, this book works with young children or family groups and is a different spin on valentine stories. Signs to use with this story: VALENTINE, MAIL, AIRPLANE, CAR/TRUCK, HAPPY

Ziefert, Harriet. *Noisy Barn!* Maplewood, N.J.: Blue Apple Books, 2003.

This large board book, with cartoony illustrations by Simms Taback, invites readers to make the noises of different farm animals. Signs to use with this story: GOAT, COW, PIG, DUCK, CHICKEN, CAT, DONKEY, BIRD, SHEEP, HORSE

Discography of Songs

Bartels, Joanie. *Bathtime Magic.* Van Nuys, Calif.: Discovery Music, 1989.

This album is chock-full of goodies for any bathtime storytime, no matter what age you're targeting. Bartels's version of "Wash Your Head Shoulders Knees and Toes" invites kids to wash each body part, and "Rub-a-Dub-Dub/Row, Row, Row Your Boat" and "The Itsy Bitsy Spider" also invite participation. Tickle parents by playing "Yellow Submarine" or "Octopus's Garden" during bubble-blowing time. Signs to use with these songs:

"Wash Your Head Shoulders Knees and Toes": WASH

"Rub-a-Dub-Dub/Row, Row, Row Your Boat": HAPPY, BOAT

Bartels, Joanie. *Christmas Magic.* Van Nuys, Calif.: Discovery Music, 1990.

Bartels offers fun, kid-friendly versions of favorite holiday songs such as "Santa Claus Is Coming to Town" and "Frosty the Snowman." Her version of "Jingle Bells" is perfect for jingling along to. Signs to use with these songs:

"Santa Claus Is Coming to Town": SANTA, COME, GOOD, BAD

"Winter Wonderland": WALK, WINTER

Bartels, Joanie. *Morning Magic*. Sherman Oaks, Calif.: Discovery Music, 1986.

This recording has several traditional morning-time songs great for sing-alongs, but the most useful for storytimes is "Wake Up Toes," a wonderful opening song that gets everyone moving. Signs to use with these songs:

"Wake Up Toes": WAKE-UP

Beall, Pamela Conn, and Susan Hagen Nipp. *Wee Sing for Baby*. Los Angeles: Price Stern Sloan, 2002.

This album contains sixty-five musical games and lullabies, but most useful for storytimes are the simplified versions found here of "Head and Shoulders," "Baby's Clothes," and "Clap Along with Me." The album also contains many useful rhymes for baby programs. Signs to use with these songs:

"Hickory Dickory Dock": CLOCK, MOUSE

"Baby's Clothes": RED, HAT, SHOES, BLUE, COAT

"The Family": MOTHER, FATHER, BROTHER, SISTER, BABY, FAMILY

Buchman, Rachel. *Hello Everybody! Playsongs and Rhymes from a Toddler's World*. Albany, New York: A Gentle Wind, 1986.

This popular storytime album contains lots of simple songs to use with toddlers. "Hello Everybody!" is a classic opening song, but don't miss the other favorites here, such as "Five Little Ducks" and "I Had a Little Rooster." "Hey Betty Martin" is an unusual and fun movement song. Though the songs are geared to toddlers, many would work just as well with preschoolers and family programs. Signs to use with these songs:

"Hello Everybody!": HELLO, YES, MOTHER, FATHER

"Five Little Ducks": DUCK, numbers 1–5

"I Had a Little Rooster": ROOSTER, COW, HORSE, CAT, BABY

"I Like to Swing": SWING

"This Is What I See": FATHER, SUN, WAKE-UP, MOTHER, GRANDMOTHER, MOON

"I Want to Wear": RED, SHOES, OVERALLS, SOCKS, COAT

"Snow Song": SNOW, WHITE, PLAY

Buchman, Rachel. *Sing a Song of Seasons*. Cambridge, Mass.: Rounder Kids, 1997.

The twenty-two tracks on this CD are ready-made for storytime, many incorporating simple actions. The songs are also divided by season. "I Went to School One Morning" is an excellent action song describing the different ways to move, while many of the other songs feature counting and offer great opportunities to introduce seasonal signs. Signs to use with these songs:

"I Went to School One Morning": SCHOOL, FATHER, LATE, HORSE, TRAIN, SLOW

"Five Little Leaves": numbers 1–5, LEAF, TREE, WIND, BROWN, RED, NONE

"I Like the Fall": FALL, OWL, GRAY, RAIN, SIT, FIRE

"Mitten Weather": MITTEN, COLD

"Let's Play in the Snow": PLAY, SNOW, COAT, HAT, SHOES, PANTS, MITTENS, COLD

"When the Pod Went Pop!": PEA
"Swimmy Swim": SWIM, WATER
"Here Is a Beehive": BEE, numbers 1–5

Coleman, Rachel de Azevedo. *Signing Time Songs, Volumes 1–3*. Salt Lake City, UT: Two Little Hands Productions, 2002.

This CD features songs from the first three volumes of the *Signing Time* video and DVD series and so includes many songs designed to reinforce basic signs. "Silly Pizza Song" is especially appropriate for storytime use and is easy to turn into a flannelboard using clip-art of various foods. "Magic Words" is a wonderful song for introducing and reinforcing signs for basic etiquette, and "Look at My Hands" is a great addition to bathtime programs. "Proud to Be Me" is a fun song to sign and dance to that also celebrates diversity. Signs to use with these songs:

"Magic Words": PLEASE, SHARE, YOUR-TURN, MY-TURN, THANK-YOU
"Look at My Hands": DIRTY, CLEAN, SOAP, WATER
"Silly Pizza Song": PIZZA, DON'T-FORGET, CHEESE, APPLE, CRACKER, ICE-CREAM, CEREAL, BREAD, COOKIE, BANANA, CANDY
"Proud to Be Me": BOY, GIRL, PROUD, ME

The Countdown Kids. *Old MacDonald Had a Farm*. Woodland Hills, Calif.: Mommy and Me, 1998.

Real kids sing these favorite songs, perfect for storytime. Signs to use with these songs:

"Old MacDonald Had a Farm": FARM, COW, CHICKEN, SHEEP, PIG, DUCK
"This Old Man": numbers 1–10
"The Farmer in the Dell": FARMER, WIFE, CHILD, NURSE, DOG, CAT, MOUSE, CHEESE, ALONE
"Bingo": DOG, B, I, N, G, O
"Here We Go Round the Mulberry Bush": days of the week
"The Big Ship Sails on the Ali-Ali-O": BOAT
"Happy Birthday": HAPPY, BIRTHDAY, YOU

Disney's Dance Along, Volume 1. Burbank, Calif.: Walt Disney Records, 1997.

This album contains kid-friendly versions of eight great dance songs, including "The Twist," "The Bunny Hop," and "The Swim." Signs to use with these songs:

"Y.M.C.A.": Y, M, C, A
"The Bunny Hop": RABBIT
"The Chicken Dance": HAPPY, SAD, CHICKEN, DANCE
"The Swim": SWIM

Greg and Steve. *We All Live Together, Volume 5*. Los Angeles: Youngheart, 1994.

"We're All Together Again" is a great opening song for any storytime. "The Number Game" is a simple, repetitive number song that would be great for reinforcing number signs one through five. "A-Walking We Will Go" provides simple movements perfect for preschool and family programs. "The Old Brass Wagon" is a circle-movement song best used with preschoolers. "Rainbow of Colors" invites children to point out objects of different colors and would be great to use with color signs. "Get Up and Go" contains all different sorts of movement, from shaking to step dancing Irish-style. "Down on the Farm" lists animal sounds on the farm, to the tune of "Wheels on the Bus." Signs to use with these songs:

"We're All Together Again": TOGETHER, HAPPY

"The Number Game": numbers 1–5

"Rainbow of Colors": RAINBOW, RED, YELLOW, BLUE, GREEN, WHITE, BROWN, ORANGE, BLACK

"Down on the Farm": ROOSTER, COW, PIG, DOG, HORSE, TURKEY, DONKEY, FARM

Groce, Larry, and the Disneyland Children's Sing-Along Chorus. *Children's Favorite Songs 3*. Burbank, Calif.: Walt Disney Records, 1990.

The version of "If You're Happy and You Know It" found here is perfect for preschool, elementary, and family programs, and this album also contains favorites such as "Itsy Bitsy Spider," "Over the River and through the Woods," and "A-Hunting We Will Go." Signs to use with these songs:

"If You're Happy and You Know It": HAPPY

"Over the River and through the Woods": GRANDMOTHER, HORSE, SNOW, WIND

Hammett, Carol, and Elaine Bueffel. *It's Toddler Time*. Long Branch, N.J.: Kimbo Educational, 1982.

This CD has many gems for baby and toddler programs, including "Clap Tap Bend," "Up, Down, Turn Around," a simple version of "If You're Happy and You Know It," and classics such as "Head Shoulders Knees and Toes" and "The Hokey Pokey." "Butterfly" is a great short song to teach the sign and invite children to dance like butterflies. Signs to use with these songs:

"If You're Happy and You Know It": HAPPY

"Butterfly": BUTTERFLY

"Little Green Apple": GREEN, APPLE, EAT/FOOD

Jump Up and Sing: Binyah's Favorite Songs (Gullah Gullah Island). Los Angeles: Kid Rhino, 1998.

This high-spirited album is full of great movement songs for storytime. "Do as I'm Doin'" invites kids to copy specific motions. "The Bajan Alphabet Song" is a great way to practice the manual alphabet, with a tune a little different from what kids are used to, while the rockin' version of "Old MacDonald" will liven up any storytime. "Move Your Body" is a great song for free dancing. The version of "If You're Happy and You Know It" found here is perfect for reinforcing emotion signs, inviting kids to "cry boo-hoo" if sad and stomp their feet if mad. "Go Underneath the Broomstick" is a great limbo song for family programs, and the jazzy "Head and Shoulders" is a fun twist on the classic song about body parts. Signs to use with these songs:

"Do as I'm Doin'": COPY

"The Bajan Alphabet Song": letters A–Z

"Old MacDonald": FARM, DUCK, COW, HORSE

"Move Your Body": DANCE

"If You're Happy and You Know It": HAPPY, SAD, MAD

Kids' Favorite Songs 2. New York: Sony Wonder, 2001.

This *Sesame Street* album features Muppet versions of classics such as "The Hokey Pokey," "This Old Man," and "The Wheels on the Bus." Don't miss Big Bird's funky version of "If You're Happy and You Know It." Signs to use with these songs:

"The More We Sing Together": TOGETHER, SING, HAPPY, FRIEND

"This Old Man": numbers 1–10

"If You're Happy and You Know It": HAPPY, GRUMPY

McGrath, Bob, and Katharine Smithram. *The Baby Record.* Teaneck, NJ: Bob's Kids Music, 2000.

This wonderful album has forty-five different bounces, rhymes, fingerplays, and songs suitable for use in baby and toddler storytimes. Play the album in programs, or just use it to learn the rhymes to present on your own. (Note: "Bubblegum" is found only on the cassette version of this album.) Signs to use with these songs:

"Bubblegum": STICKY, CHEWING-GUM

"As I Was Walking to Town One Day": DOG, CAT, DUCK, COW

"One Is a Giant": BALL, numbers 1–4

Palmer, Hap. *"So Big": Activity Songs for Little Ones.* Topanga, Calif.: Hap-Pal Music, 1994.

Palmer's gentle songs are great for baby and toddler programs, and the "Rock and Roll Freeze Dance" is great for all ages. This album contains many great movement songs, such as "When I'm Down I Get Up and Dance," "Teddy Bear Playtime," and "Put Your Hands in the Air." Signs to use with these songs:

"So Happy You're Here": HAPPY, HERE

"Five Little Monkeys": numbers 1–5, MONKEY, MOTHER, THINK

Raffi. *The Corner Grocery Store.* Willowdale, Ontario: Shoreline, 1979.

This CD is full of great songs for teaching food signs, from "Cluck, Cluck, Red Hen" to "Popcorn" to "Going on a Picnic." Signs to use with these songs:

"Cluck, Cluck, Red Hen": SHEEP, CHICKEN, EGG, COW, MILK, BEE, HONEY

"Popcorn": HOT, POPCORN

"Going on a Picnic": RAIN, SANDWICH, SALAD, MELON, APPLE, DRINK, COOKIE

Raffi. *More Singable Songs.* Willowdale, Ontario: Troubadour Records, 1977.

More great action songs for storytime here, including "Six Little Ducks," "You Gotta Sing," and, of course, "Shake My Sillies Out." Signs to use with these songs:

"Six Little Ducks": number 6, DUCK

"You Gotta Sing": SING/MUSIC, SHOUT, PLAY

Raffi. *One Light, One Sun.* Hollywood, Calif.: A&M Records, 1985.

"Time to Sing" is a wonderful opening song for any storytime. "In My Garden" is a great action song for gardening programs, while "Down on Grandpa's Farm" lists animals and their sounds. Raffi's versions of classics such as "Octopus's Garden," "Apples and Bananas," "Take Me Out to the Ballgame," and "Twinkle Twinkle Little Star" are also great for storytimes. Signs to use with these songs:

"Time to Sing": HELLO

"Down on Grandpa's Farm": COW, CHICKEN, SHEEP, DOG, HORSE

Raffi. *Singable Songs for the Very Young*. Hollywood, Calif.: A&M Records, 1976.

Raffi's classic collection has lots of great songs for storytime, including the ultimate opening song, "The More We Get Together," and other favorites such as "Five Little Frogs," "Bumping Up and Down," "Spider on the Floor," and "Mr. Sun." Signs to use with these songs:

"The More We Get Together": MORE, TOGETHER, HAPPY, FRIEND

"Five Little Frogs": numbers 1–5, GREEN, FROG, BUG

"Willoughby Wallaby Woo": ELEPHANT

"Going to the Zoo": Z-O-O (spelled), MOTHER, MONKEY, CROCODILE

"Five Little Pumpkins": numbers 1–5, PUMPKIN

"The Sharing Song": MINE, SHARE, FOOD, BOOK

"Mr. Sun": SUN, TREE, PLAY

Scruggs, Joe. *Late Last Night*. Austin, Tex.: Educational Graphics Press, 1998.

This CD is full of great action songs for preschool, family, and even elementary programs. The title track invites kids to do the actions connected with various types of footwear, including motorcycle boots, space boots, and ice skates. "Wiggle in My Toe" follows a wiggle through the whole body and is a great action song for older kids. "Ants in My Pants" and "Turn Around Game" are also great action songs for storytime. Signs to use with these songs:

"Late Last Night": DANCE, SHOE, SKATE, ASTRONAUT, SWIM, MOTORCYCLE, HOT, COWBOY, INDIAN, BASEBALL

Sharon, Lois, and Bram. *The Elephant Show, Volume 1*. Los Angeles: Drive Entertainment, 1986.

This album features favorite songs from the TV show, including many great action songs, such as "Chugga Chugga." Signs to use with these songs:

"One Elephant Went Out to Play": 1, 2, ELEPHANT, PLAY

"Everybody Happy?": days of the week

"On a Picnic We Will Go": SUMMER, HOT-DOGS, CORN, NUT, BLANKET, FRISBEE, BASEBALL, WATERMELON

"Ten in the Bed": numbers 1–10, BED

Sharon, Lois, and Bram. *Great Big Hits 2*. Toronto: Elephant Records, 2002.

The traditional "Tommy Thumb" is a wonderful finger-game song to use in baby programs. Use "Bingo" to reinforce the manual alphabet in a fun way. This album also contains great movement songs and classics such as "Hokey Pokey" and "Name Game." Signs to use with these songs:

"Everybody Happy?": days of the week

"Bingo": DOG, B, I, N, G, O

"Name Game": NAME, letters A–Z

Sharon, Lois, and Bram. *Mainly Mother Goose*. Toronto: Elephant Records, 1984.

This album is full of nursery rhymes and songs based on classic Mother Goose rhymes. The version of "The Eensy Weensy Spider" found here, which covers the regular-sized, great big, and teeny tiny spider, is a favorite storytime activity song to use with any age group. Signs to use with these songs:

"Five Green Apples": FARMER, GREEN, APPLE, EAT/FOOD, numbers 1–5

Splish Splash: Bath Time Fun. New York: Sony Wonder, 1995.

This *Sesame Street* CD is full of great songs for bathtime programs, from classics such as "Splish Splash" and "Rubber Duckie" to fun favorites such as the reggae-inspired "Do de Rubber Duck." "Everybody Wash" is an especially good activity song for all ages. Signs to use with these songs:

"Everybody Wash": WASH

APPENDIX C

Games and Crafts to
Use in ASL Programs

All My Neighbors

Ages: Six and up

Purpose: To reinforce color and clothing signs

Materials and advance preparation required: Set up chairs or carpet squares in a circle, with one fewer than the number of players.

Signs used: Color signs, clothing signs

Directions: Players sit down, with one player standing in the middle. The player in the middle signs a color, item of clothing, or color/clothing item combination (e.g., RED, SHOE, or RED SHOE), and all players who are wearing that color or item must stand up and find a new place. The player in the middle must try to steal a seat. Whichever player does not get a seat becomes the new middle person and must sign something new.

The Alphabet Game

Ages: Six and up

Purpose: To reinforce the manual alphabet

Materials and advance preparation required: None

Signs used: Letters A–Z

Directions: Have players stand in a circle. The player to your right chooses a letter and signs it without speaking. Players in the circle raise their hands if they know the letter and, when called on, must give a word that begins with that letter. The player who supplied the word then signs another letter.

Charades

Ages: Six and up
Purpose: To encourage use of gestures and creative thinking
Materials and advance preparation required: None
Signs used: None (gestures only)
Directions: This is a great icebreaker activity that can be adapted for different program themes. Divide participants into pairs, encouraging them to meet someone new. Ask them to turn their voices off and find out each other's favorite animal, food, or sports activity. Ask each pair to sit down once they have finished, and when everyone is done, go around the circle and have each player announce his or her partner's favorite thing and how he or she figured it out. Use this activity to discuss the many different ways one could act out the same idea.

Colorful Squares

Ages: Eight and up
Purpose: To reinforce color signs
Materials and advance preparation required: Make squares of construction paper or posterboard in red, yellow, orange, green, blue, purple, pink, and black, with enough so that each player can have one to three colors, depending on your age group. (If you plan to use these squares more than once, you may want to laminate them.) Set up carpet squares or chairs in a circle, with one fewer than you have players.
Signs used: RED, ORANGE, YELLOW, GREEN, BLUE, PURPLE, PINK, BLACK, RAINBOW
Directions: Have everyone sit in a circle and review the color signs. Give each person one to three color squares. This is a voices-off game. The person in the middle signs a color (it does not have to be the color of one of his or her squares). Make sure that the person in the middle turns and signs the color several times, so everyone can see it. Everyone in the circle who has that color must get up and find a new seat. The center person tries to steal one of the empty seats. Whichever player is left without a seat must go to the middle and sign another color. Players may also choose to sign RAINBOW, which means that everyone must get up and find a new seat.

Deaf Culture True and False

Ages: Eight and up
Purpose: To dispel myths about deaf people and deafness

Materials and advance preparation required: List the statements provided here on index cards. If you plan to use the cards in multiple programs, you may want to laminate them.

Signs used: TRUE, FALSE

Directions: Teach the signs for TRUE and FALSE. Give each participant a card. Go around the room and have each person read the statement on his or her card. Ask everyone to consider the statement and then sign whether they think it is TRUE or FALSE. Discuss each point using the notes accompanying each statement.

Deaf people can drive. (TRUE. In fact, some studies have shown that deaf people tend to be better drivers, in general, than hearing people because deaf drivers are more visual.)

Deaf people can enjoy music. (TRUE. Deaf people have different degrees of hearing. Some deaf people may be able to hear some musical ranges, and all deaf people can enjoy vibrations of music. Drums are popular within the deaf community.)

All deaf people communicate using their hands. (FALSE. Many deaf people communicate using sign language, but others may prefer speechreading, voice, or a combination of methods.)

Deaf people cannot go to college. (FALSE. Deaf people can go to college just like anyone else. Deaf people can choose to go to a hearing school and use an interpreter or go to a school such as Gallaudet University in Washington, D.C., where the classes are taught in ASL.)

Hearing impaired is a nicer term than *deaf*. (FALSE. Many deaf people do not consider themselves disabled, and so to call them "impaired" is an insult. They simply use a different language. Some deaf people say that they're not "hearing impaired"—hearing people are just "signing impaired"!)

All deaf people wear hearing aids. (FALSE. Some deaf people use hearing aids, and some choose not to.)

Hearing aids allow deaf people to hear just as much as hearing people do. (FALSE. Depending on how much hearing a deaf person has, a hearing aid may or may not help him or her. Sometimes a hearing aid will help to hear some background noises, but a deaf person will still rely on sign language or speechreading to communicate.)

If you meet a deaf person, you should shout so he or she can hear you. (FALSE. Most deaf people won't be able to hear you clearly enough to understand you even if you shout, and besides, would you really want people shouting at you?)

Deaf people go to school. (TRUE. Deaf people go to school just as hearing people do. Some deaf children go to public schools, with an interpreter in the classroom. Some deaf children go to schools for the deaf, where the teachers sign.)

All deaf people can read lips. (FALSE. Most movies that feature deaf people show them reading lips, but the fact is that speechreading—the proper term for it—is usually easier for hearing people than for deaf people! Speechreading takes a long time to learn and requires looking not only at the lips but also at the throat and face, as well as considering the context of a conversation.)

If a deaf person is trying to read your lips, it's a good idea to speak very slowly and enunciate every word very carefully. (FALSE. If someone is trying to read your lips, speak normally—not too slowly, not too quickly. Stretching your mouth or overenunciating makes it very hard to understand you.)

Deaf people read braille. (FALSE. Braille is a system of raised dots designed for blind people. Deaf people read printed words, just like hearing people.)

Deaf people are also dumb. (FALSE. You might hear older people, especially, use the phrase "deaf and dumb." This comes from an old-fashioned meaning of the word *dumb*: "can't speak." Of course, we know now that deaf people *can* speak, so even that old meaning is wrong!)

Deaf people are quiet. (FALSE. Deaf people can be just as noisy as hearing people.)

Deaf people can learn as much as anyone else. (TRUE. Deaf people go to school just as hearing people do and can learn as much as hearing people can.)

Deaf people can't speak. (FALSE. Deaf people have the ability to speak, just like hearing people. However, it's hard to learn to pronounce words you have never heard. Some deaf people prefer not to use their voices at all, and some speak very clearly.)

Sign language is universal. (FALSE. Just as spoken language is not universal, neither is sign language. There are many different sign languages throughout the world, including American Sign Language, French Sign Language, and Chinese Sign Language.)

Deaf people can become bosses or supervisors. (TRUE. Deaf people can achieve just about anything hearing people can.)

If you're talking to a deaf person through an interpreter, you should talk directly to the deaf person. (TRUE. Look at and speak directly to the deaf person, and pretend the interpreter isn't there. It's rude to say things such as, "Tell her I said hello.")

Deaf people can't go to the movies. (FALSE. Many theaters run special open-captioned shows of popular movies, where captions of the dialogue and other sound information are projected on the bottom on the screen.)

Drawing Shapes

Ages: Six and up

Purpose: To encourage visual attention and perception

Materials and advance preparation required: Paper and pencil for each player, blackboard and chalk or flipchart and markers, predrawn shapes for presenter

Signs used: None

Directions: The leader silently draws shapes in the air, which participants must then draw on their papers. Repeat each shape until everyone thinks they know what it is, then invite a volunteer to come and draw it on the board. Show the shape again so that everyone can see it. Begin with simple shapes, such as circles and triangles, then move to complicated designs such as three triangles stacked on top of each other, or the shape of a shield. (Stick to symmetrical shapes, unless you are well versed in ASL, because directionality is a separate issue in ASL and may cause confusion here.)

Drawing Shapes: Color Variation

Ages: Six and up

Purpose: To encourage visual attention and perception and to reinforce color signs

Materials and advance preparation required: Paper and pencil for each player, blackboard and chalk or flipchart and markers, predrawn shapes for presenter. You may also wish to provide crayons or markers in different colors.

Signs used: Color signs

Directions: Follow the directions for the previous activity (Drawing Shapes), but add a colorful twist by pointing to various parts of the shape and signing what color it is. Participants may either write the color on their papers in that part of the shape or use crayons or markers to color it.

Fingerspelling Circle

Ages: Eight and up

Purpose: To reinforce the manual alphabet

Materials and advance preparation required: None

Signs used: Letters A–Z

Directions: Have all players sit in a circle. Start by fingerspelling a short word (three to five letters). The player to your right then must fingerspell a word that begins with the last letter of your word. For example, if you spell C-A-T, the next player might spell T-E-A-R. The next player then spells a word that begins with the last letter of the second player's word, and so on. Decide in advance whether players will be allowed to repeat words already used or use proper names.

Go Fish with Names

Ages: Nine and up
Purpose: To reinforce the manual alphabet, both expressively and receptively
Materials and advance preparation required: Write simple three- to four-letter names, such as Tom, May, and Evan, on fifty-two index cards, using each name twice. If you plan to use these cards more than once, you may want to laminate them.
Signs used: YOU, HAVE, letters A–Z, YES, NO, GO, FISHING
Directions: Shuffle the cards and distribute seven to each player. Place the rest of the deck in the middle of the players. Teach the signs used in this game, then have everyone turn their voices off. The first player may ask any player, using signs, if he or she has a particular name. If that player has it, he or she must give it up, but if not, he or she signs NO or GO FISHING. If the first player gets a pair, he or she puts it down on the table and takes another turn. If the first player does not get a pair, he or she must choose from the pile in the middle. This continues until everyone has matched all their cards, and the player with the most pairs wins.

Handshape Pins

Ages: Ten and up
Purpose: To reinforce the manual alphabet and the I-LOVE-YOU sign
Materials and advance preparation required: Foam shapes of hands (available in most craft stores), pin backings, tacky glue, clothespins.
Signs used: Letters A–Z, I-LOVE-YOU
Directions: Shape foam hands into manual letters or I-LOVE-YOU signs and glue into place with tacky glue. Use the clothespins to hold the foam in place while it dries (this can take thirty to fifty minutes). Glue a pin backing to the back of the hand.

I Went to the Zoo

Ages: Eight and up

Purpose: To reinforce animal signs, memory, and visual attention

Materials and advance preparation required: None

Signs used: I, GO, Z-O-O (spelled), SEE, animal signs of your choice

Directions: Participants sit in a circle for this voices-off game. The first player signs I GO Z-O-O, SEE and an animal sign. The second player must then repeat this phrase and add another animal. The third player must repeat the phrase, signing both of the other animals and adding another. This continues until someone misses an animal, in which case he or she is out. Continue until there is only one player left, who is the winner.

I-L-Y Flowers

Ages: Six and up

Purpose: To reinforce the sign I-LOVE-YOU

Materials and advance preparation required: Cut various colors of construction paper or craft foam in half. Provide each participant with one flowerpot, three or four construction paper or craft foam halves, three or four straws, a square of floral foam, Spanish moss or other floral filler, scissors, a pencil, and glue.

Signs used: I-LOVE-YOU

Directions: Have each participant trace his or her hand onto the construction paper or craft foam to make three or four "flowers." Cut out the hands, and glue down the middle and ring fingers to make the I-LOVE-YOU sign. Then glue the "flowers" to the straws, and stick the straws into the floral foam. Arrange the floral foam in the flowerpots and cover with filler. Participants may also decorate the flowerpots with markers, paint, or stickers.

I-L-Y Stick Puppets

Ages: Three and up

Purpose: To reinforce the sign I-LOVE-YOU

Materials and advance preparation required: Provide each participant with construction paper or posterboard, scissors, a pencil, a tongue depressor or craft stick, and glue. For younger children, you may wish to provide precut handshapes.

Signs used: I-LOVE-YOU

Directions: Have each participant trace his or her hand onto the construction paper or posterboard. Cut out the hand, and glue down the middle and ring fingers to make the I-LOVE-YOU sign. Then glue the handshape to a craft stick or tongue depressor. Participants may also decorate the handshapes with crayons, markers, or stickers.

Mirror Game

Ages: Eight and up
Purpose: To encourage visual discrimination
Materials and advance preparation required: None
Signs used: None
Directions: Divide participants into pairs and have each pair face each other. Designate a leader. The leader must make different motions, such as raising an arm, moving a leg, and so on. The follower must try to be the leader's mirror image. After a while, have the participants switch roles.

Moose

Ages: Eight and up
Purpose: To reinforce animal signs and visual attention
Materials and advance preparation: List of animal signs. You may wish to have children pick from a list of signs during the game.
Signs used: MOOSE, MOUSE, animal signs of your choice
Directions: All participants sit in a circle. The leader is the moose, and the player to the left of the leader is the mouse. The other players each choose an animal sign. Review the animal signs and the rules of the game, and then have everyone turn their voices off. The leader begins by signing MOOSE plus one other animal. The person with that animal must sign his animal, plus one other. Play should continue in a rhythm. Keep going until someone misses his or her turn, either by throwing the rhythm off, failing to sign their animal, or not signing a new animal quickly enough. That person becomes the mouse, and the mouse moves one place over to become the moose, and everyone else moves over to fill in the spaces. Continue with the new animals assigned to those spaces. This game is a bit complicated but a great favorite with elementary and middle school kids, who pick it up quickly.

My Mother Ate . . .

Ages: Eight and up
Purpose: To reinforce food signs, memory, and visual attention

Materials and advance preparation required: None

Signs used: MY, MOTHER, EAT/FOOD, food signs of your choice

Directions: Participants sit in a circle for this voices-off game. The first player signs MY MOTHER EAT and a food sign. The second player must then repeat this phrase and add another food. The third player must repeat the phrase, signing both of the other foods and adding another. This continues until someone misses a food, in which case he or she is out. Continue until there is only one player left, who is the winner.

Name Plaques

Ages: Eight and up

Purpose: To reinforce the manual alphabet

Materials and advance preparation required: Photocopy the manual alphabet from an ASL book, making sure that you have multiple copies of often-used letters such as A, E, S, and T. Cut the letters out and mix them up. (You may wish to keep vowels and consonants separate.) Provide each participant with a piece of construction paper or posterboard and a glue stick, as well as crayons, markers, or stickers to use as decorations. Put up a large poster or transparency of the manual alphabet to help participants identify the letters.

Signs used: Letters A–Z, NAME

Directions: Each child must find the letters of his or her name and glue them onto the posterboard or construction paper. Children may also decorate their papers with crayons, markers, or stickers.

Pass the Colors

Ages: Six and up

Purpose: To reinforce color and direction signs

Materials and advance preparation required: Make squares of construction paper or posterboard in red, yellow, orange, green, blue, purple, pink, and black, with enough so that each player can have one to three colors, depending on your age group. If you plan to use these more than once, you may want to laminate them.

Signs used: RED, ORANGE, YELLOW, GREEN, BLUE, PURPLE, PINK, BLACK, RAINBOW, RIGHT, LEFT

Directions: Have players sit in a circle. Review the signs used in this game, then give each player two or three color squares. This is a voices-off game. The leader signs a color and then RIGHT or LEFT, and the players who have that color must pass it to the persons on their right or left. The leader may occasionally sign RAINBOW, which means all colors must be passed. Continue until one or two people have all the colors, or the group is sick of the game, whichever comes first. Whoever ends up with the most squares at the end of the game is the winner.

Pass the Food

Ages: Eight and up
Purpose: To encourage visual discrimination and use of gestures
Materials and advance preparation required: None
Signs used: None (gestures only)
Directions: Everyone sits in a circle. Explain that you have a magic bag full of different kinds of food and that you will take each item out and pass it around. This is a voices-off game, so players will have to watch carefully to see how you handle each item and guess what it is. As you pass the item, each player should handle it and interact with it in an appropriate way. This game can be a lot of fun and a wonderful icebreaker, especially for older kids. Once each item goes all the way around the circle, ask what it is. Suggestions for items: egg, pitcher of water, watermelon, bubble gum, hot potato, ice cube, pizza

Same and Different

Ages: Eight and up
Purpose: To encourage visual discrimination
Materials and advance preparation required: Predrawn shapes or lists of signs for presenter
Signs used: SAME, DIFFERENT
Directions: Draw two shapes in the air, one to your left and one to your right. Participants must determine whether the shapes are the same or different, then sign the appropriate response. Vary whether the shapes are the same or different as you progress through the game. This game can also be used with fingerspelled words, numbers, simple signs, and full sentences, or use it to reinforce the importance of facial grammar by signing phrases that differ only by facial expression (e.g., YOUR NAME K-A-T-E versus YOUR NAME K-A-T-E?).

Silent Birthday Line-Up

Ages: Nine and up
Purpose: To explore nonverbal communication and encourage creative thinking
Materials and advance preparation required: None
Signs used: None (gestures only)
Directions: Ask participants to line up in order of their birthdays, specifying only that they are not allowed to talk to each other to find out where they fit in the line. Once they have finished lining up, discuss the ways they communicated or could have communicated: signing, fingerspelling, writing, gesturing, air writing, and so on.

The Story of ASL

Ages: Nine and up
Purpose: To teach basic signs while sharing the history of American Sign Language
Materials and advance preparation required: Print out pictures of Laurent Clerc and Thomas Hopkins Gallaudet (available at http://clerccenter .gallaudet.edu/Literacy/MSSDLRC/clerc/index.html) to show as you tell this story.
Signs used: DEAF, HEARING, SIGN, LANGUAGE, SCHOOL, NO, AMERICA, YES, READ, WRITE
Directions: Show the pictures and demonstrate signs for the words in capital letters as you tell the following story:

About two hundred years ago, there were no schools for DEAF people in the United States. In fact, most DEAF people lived very far apart from each other, so they didn't even use the same language. Most DEAF people had HEARING parents, so they couldn't learn SIGN LANGUAGE from their parents. A wealthy doctor had a daughter who was DEAF, and he wanted to open a school so that she and other DEAF children would have a place to go. So he asked his neighbor, Reverend Thomas Hopkins Gallaudet, to help him start the school. Gallaudet decided to go to England to learn about deaf education there. But when he got to the SCHOOL there, which used speechreading instead of SIGN LANGUAGE, they said NO, they would not share their information with him. So he was stuck.

At that time, the head of the school for the deaf in Paris was in England. He and two of the teachers at the school, who were both DEAF, were giving lectures to help raise money for their SCHOOL. Thomas Gallaudet went to one of these lectures, and afterward he went up and introduced himself. The men were delighted to help him, and they invited him to come back with them to France to learn about their methods. One of the DEAF teachers was Laurent Clerc.

Gallaudet stayed in Paris for several months, learning all he could. He was fascinated by the French SIGN LANGUAGE used at the school. But then he was called home to AMERICA, and he realized there was still a lot left to learn. So he asked Laurent Clerc to come back to AMERICA with him and help him start the SCHOOL. Laurent Clerc said YES, and the two of them got on the ship for AMERICA. It was a long journey, and on the way, Gallaudet taught Clerc to READ and WRITE English, and Clerc taught Gallaudet French SIGN LANGUAGE.

The SCHOOL opened in 1817 in Hartford, Connecticut, and it is still open today. Now it is called the AMERICAN SCHOOL for the DEAF. When Clerc first started teaching, there was no such thing as AMERICAN SIGN LANGUAGE. He used a combination of French SIGN LAN-GUAGE and the SIGNS that the students brought with them to the SCHOOL. This turned into what we now know as AMERICAN SIGN LANGUAGE. Even today, ASL has a lot of signs in common with French SIGN LANGUAGE, all because of Laurent Clerc.

Something terrible happened in 1880—there was a big conference about DEAF education in Milan, Italy. For some reason, people at this confer-ence decided that SIGN LANGUAGE was bad and that DEAF people shouldn't be allowed to use it. So all the DEAF teachers were fired, and students were not allowed to use SIGN LANGUAGE in the classroom. Imagine that! Suppose your teacher came into the classroom tomorrow and said, "From now on I am only going to teach you in Chinese, and if you don't understand me, too bad." That's just what it was like for the DEAF kids.

Now remember, most DEAF people have HEARING parents. So where do you think they learned SIGN LANGUAGE if they couldn't learn it at SCHOOL? Well, those few DEAF kids who had DEAF parents brought it with them from home, and they used it in the dormitories and outside the classroom, and sometimes the DEAF teachers who had been taken out of the classroom also worked in the dormitories. So basically, AMERICAN SIGN LANGUAGE survived underground for about eighty years! Finally, in the 1960s, a linguist started studying ASL, and he proved that it is just as complex and unique as any spoken LANGUAGE. Now, most

SCHOOLS for DEAF students use SIGN LANGUAGE, and we know that AMERICAN SIGN LANGUAGE is a beautiful language!

TTY

Ages: Six and up

Purpose: To encourage visual discrimination and reinforce key vocabulary

Materials and advance preparation required: Select a list of signs, phrases, or sentences relating to your program (e.g., food signs, animal signs, fingerspelled words).

Signs used: Your choice

Directions: This game is a voices-off sign language variation of the old classic game of Telephone. Have players line up facing away from you so that each player is facing the back of the person in front of him or her. Tap the first person in line on the shoulder, and have him or her turn around. Sign a sign, phrase, or sentence to this person. Then he or she turns and taps the next person on the shoulder, who turns around. The first person signs the information to that person, who taps the next person and passes it on, and so on. When the final person in line gets the sign, he or she signs it for the whole group, and they compare it with the original message.

Who's the Leader?

Ages: Eight and up

Purpose: To encourage visual discrimination

Materials and advance preparation required: None

Signs used: None

Directions: This is a wonderful voices-off icebreaker game, and groups of various ages find it fun. Have everyone stand in a circle, and send one person, the guesser, out of the room. Silently choose one person to be the leader. The leader begins an action, such as tapping his or her head or doing a funky dance move, which everyone else must copy. Call the guesser back into the room. The guesser stands in the middle of the circle and tries to figure out who the leader is. The other players should be careful not to watch the leader too obviously. The leader must change the movement every thirty seconds or so. The guesser guesses until correct, and then the leader becomes the next guesser to go outside, and another leader is chosen.

APPENDIX D

Glossary of Terms Relating to Sign Language and Deafness

ADA: Acronym for the Americans with Disabilities Act.

American Sign Language: The sign language used by most deaf people in the United States and Canada.

Americans with Disabilities Act: The law passed in 1990 that provides for accommodations for people with a variety of disabilities in all public services. Titles II and III of this act require state and local governments, public accommodations, and commercial facilities to provide reasonable accommodations for communication.

Ameslan: An older shorthand term for American Sign Language, used in the 1970s and 1980s. The acronym *ASL* is much preferred today.

ASL: A commonly used acronym for American Sign Language.

bilingual biculturalism: The paradigm of deaf education that came into favor in the 1990s, which favors treating ASL and English as separate but equal languages and presents hearing and Deaf cultures with equal respect. The language of instruction is generally ASL, with English emphasized in reading and writing.

Clerc, Laurent (1785–1869): The first deaf teacher in the United States and in the entire western hemisphere. Clerc was educated at the Institut Royal des Sourds-Muets (Royal Institution for the Deaf) in Paris, where he became a teacher at age twenty. In 1816, Clerc accompanied Thomas Hopkins Gallaudet to the United States to help found the Connecticut Asylum at Hartford for the Education and Instruction of Deaf and Dumb Persons. Because Clerc taught using French Sign Language, FSL became one of the vital ingredients of American Sign Language.

cochlear implant: An electronic device, implanted in the skull, that bypasses the external and middle ears. Sounds are picked up by means of a microphone connected to a processor worn externally. The processor converts the sounds to electronic impulses, which are sent to the implanted radio receiver via a transmitting coil worn behind the ear and attached to the head via magnets. The signals are then sent to the implant, which stimulates the auditory nerve. The auditory nerve sends the impulses to the brain, where they are interpreted as sound. Cochlear implants are the subject of much debate in the deaf community.

Connecticut Asylum at Hartford for the Education and Instruction of Deaf and Dumb Persons: The first school for the deaf in the United States, which opened on April 15, 1817. Considered to be the birthplace of ASL, the school is still in operation today as the American School for the Deaf.

deaf: A general term referring to hearing loss.

Deaf: Relating to Deaf Culture.

deaf community: The community of deaf people and users of American Sign Language.

Deaf Culture: The collections of beliefs and values that form the core of the deaf community, including the primacy of ASL, the belief that deaf people are not disabled, and the shared experience of deafness.

deaf-blind: Refers to loss of both hearing and sight, partial or total. Deaf-blindness can be caused by a variety of factors, and age of onset usually determines preferred communication method and whether a deaf-blind person identifies more with the Deaf or hearing world.

freelance interpreter: An interpreter who works as a free agent, instead of through an agency, and may be contracted directly.

French Sign Language: The language used by most deaf people in France. Laurent Clerc brought this language to America in 1816, and it combined with Martha's Vineyard Sign Language and students' home signs at the Connecticut Asylum at Hartford for the Education and Instruction of Deaf and Dumb Persons to form American Sign Language. Even today, many similarities between ASL and FSL are evident.

Gallaudet, Thomas Hopkins (1787–1851): With Laurent Clerc and Dr. Mason Fitch Cogswell, a founder of the first school for the deaf in the United States and a staunch advocate of the use of sign language in deaf education.

Gallaudet University: The only liberal arts college for deaf people in the world. Classes are taught in ASL. The school was originally incorporated in 1857 as the Columbia Institution for the Instruction of the Deaf and Dumb and the Blind. Dr. Edward Miner Gallaudet, son of Thomas Hopkins Gallaudet, was the school's first superintendent. In 1893, at the request of the alumni association, the school was renamed Gallaudet College in honor of Thomas Hopkins Gallaudet. For more information, see www.gallaudet.edu.

Gestuno: Also known as International Sign Language, this limited set of established signs, supplemented by gestures, is used to interpret at international conferences of the deaf.

glossing: A system of representing American Sign Language using the English words most closely equivalent to the ASL signs. Glosses are written in capital letters, and the English words are hyphenated when more than one word is required to represent an ASL sign.

handshape: One of the five sign parameters identified by linguists. Each sign has a particular handshape, and changing that handshape changes the meaning of the sign. Just as English contains a limited number of sounds, each sign language contains a limited number of handshapes.

hard of hearing: Having some degree of hearing loss. Depending on their cultural and language orientation, hard-of-hearing people may consider themselves part of the hearing or Deaf world, or may go back and forth between the two.

hearing aid: A device worn on the ear to amplify sound. Hearing aids generally assist with hearing environmental sounds and build on any hearing a person already has. Some deaf people use hearing aids as a supplement to speechreading; some deaf people find they do not work for them at all.

hearing culture: Mainstream culture that usually views deafness as a disability.

hearing impaired: A term often used for deafness in the hearing community. Some think the term is more politically correct, when in actuality, many deaf people find the term offensive, with its implications of brokenness.

home signs: Made-up signs that hold meaning only within a given family or social unit.

International Sign Language: A name often used for Gestuno, an established set of signs used at international conferences of the deaf.

interpreter: A professional who facilitates communication between two different languages. An interpreter must be skilled in both languages as well as the process of interpretation itself.

interpreting agency: An agency that provides interpreting services for clients. Advantages of using an agency to book interpreters include quality control and convenience. Interpreting agencies charge a fee for their services in procuring the interpreter, as well as the fee for the interpreting service itself.

lipreading: An inaccurate term often used for speechreading.

location: One of the five sign parameters identified by linguists. Each sign is performed in a specific location; changing that location changes the meaning of the sign.

manual alphabet: A set of handshapes used to represent the letters of a written language in a sign language. The American manual alphabet contains twenty-six handshapes that correspond with the English alphabet. Though knowing the manual alphabet is invaluable for representing English words such as names, brand names, and proper nouns in signed form, the manual alphabet is not ASL.

Martha's Vineyard Sign Language: The sign language used by both hearing and deaf people for more than two hundred years on the island of Martha's Vineyard, where 1 in every 155 people was born deaf. When the first school for the deaf in the United States opened in 1817, students from the island brought their language to the school, where it mixed with French Sign Language and various home signs to form what we know as American Sign Language.

Milan Congress: The 1880 education conference held in Milan, Italy, which declared the supremacy of the oral method in teaching deaf students and led to the decline of the manual method of instruction in schools for the deaf around the world.

movement: One of the five sign parameters identified by linguists. Each sign has a specific movement, and changing that movement changes the meaning of the sign.

NAD: Acronym for the National Association of the Deaf.

National Association of the Deaf: The national organization whose mission is "to promote, protect, and preserve the rights and quality of life of deaf and hard of hearing individuals in the United States of America." NAD is a leading advocate for technology, captioning, and legal rights of deaf individuals. For more information, see www.nad.org.

nonmanual signals: One of the five sign parameters identified by linguists and arguably the most important. Nonmanual signals encompass all parts of a sign that are not on the hands, including facial expression, mouth movements, and body shifting. Much as an utterance in English can be entirely changed based on tone of voice, nonmanual signals often trump all other parts of a sign in determining meaning.

oralism: The belief that the oral method of instruction—using speechreading and speech—is superior to the manual method, which uses sign language, gestures, and other visual means.

palm orientation: One of the five sign parameters identified by linguists.

Palm orientation refers to which way the palm faces during the production of a sign. Each sign has a specific palm orientation, and if that orientation changes, so too does the meaning of the sign.

parameters: The term given to the distinct parts of a sign by linguists. Parameters are comparable to morphemes and phonemes, the building blocks of spoken languages. William Stokoe originally identified three parameters (movement, location, and handshape); later researchers added palm orientation and nonmanual signals to the list.

processing time: Required by interpreters to provide an accurate interpretation of the message. Because an interpreter requires time to process the original message and interpret into the target language, the interpreter will always be a bit behind the first speaker or signer.

regional variation in ASL: The use of different signs in different parts of the country for the same concepts. Regional variation in ASL is comparable to regional variation in English; however, it may be slightly more pronounced because ASL does not have the widespread standardization brought on by the media that English has.

Registry of Interpreters for the Deaf: The national organization that certifies and advocates for American Sign Language interpreters in the United States. For more information, see www.rid.org.

RID: Acronym for the Registry of Interpreters for the Deaf.

RID Code of Ethics: The voluntary code of ethics that RID-certified interpreters agree to uphold. The tenets of the code of ethics include maintaining confidentiality, providing impartial interpretation, maintaining professional development, and practicing discretion in selecting assignments. For more information, see www.rid.org/coe.html.

Sicard, Abbé Roche Ambrose (1742–1822): Head of the Institut Royal des Sourds-Muets (Royal Institution for the Deaf) in Paris, France, from 1790 to 1822. Thomas Hopkins Gallaudet attended a lecture given by Sicard and two of his students during his 1815 trip to England, and Sicard invited Gallaudet back to Paris, where he could learn about the school's methods using sign language in education. This trip led to the establishment of the first permanent school for the deaf in the United States, as well as the use of the manual method in that school.

sign language: A language that uses the visual and manual modes rather than the auditory and spoken modes. Hundreds of sign languages exist throughout the world, and few if any have any correlation to the spoken language in their respective countries.

Signed English: An attempt to represent English in a manual form. In the 1960s and 1970s, many different systems were developed using some ASL signs, in English word order, along with artificial signs to represent suffixes such as "ing," which are unnecessary in ASL. These systems, among them manually coded English and Signing Exact English, were developed by educators in an attempt to expose deaf children to English structure. However, most failed as true means of communication because they ignored the unique visual aspects of ASL and advocated the use of one sign for every English word, giving primacy to English vocabulary instead of conceptual meanings.

sim-com: A shorthand term for "simultaneous communication," or the attempt to use both signed and spoken language at the same time. Because of the completely different structures of ASL and English, it is impossible to use both languages at the same time, and so attempts to sustain sim-com usually result in a jumble that isn't quite either language.

speechreading: A complex process that attempts to decode spoken language through a visual mode. Truly skilled speechreaders are rare; they use a variety of cues such as the throat and facial muscle movement, facial expression, and contextual knowledge to determine meaning.

spoken language: A language that uses the auditory and spoken modes.

Stokoe, William (1919–2000): Linguist whose studies of American Sign Language led to a complete shift in the way sign languages were understood and the gradual reemergence of sign language as the basis of education for deaf children. Stokoe's *Sign Language Structure*, published in 1960, broke down the elements of ASL just as other linguists had previously broken down the structure of spoken languages.

tactile signing: Communication method often used by deaf-blind individuals. Famously used by Helen Keller, tactile signing involves the use of ASL in the receiving person's hand. Some modifications of visual features of ASL are required in tactile signing (e.g., when asking a question, which is usually evident by facial expression, a tactile signer must sign QUESTION because the recipient of the message cannot see the signer's face).

total communication: An educational theory that emerged in the 1970s that espoused the use of whichever communication method (sign, voice, or both) best meets a child's needs. While the theoretical basis of the theory is sound, in actuality it often means that a teacher uses sim-com, or both signs and speech, in the classroom, which deprives profoundly deaf students of exposure to true ASL.

Usher's syndrome: A condition in which children are born deaf and gradually lose their sight later in life, usually beginning in the teen years. Because Usher's syndrome is one of the leading causes of deaf-blindness, many deaf-blind people grow up in the deaf community using ASL and naturally progress to tactile signing as their sight decreases.

APPENDIX E

Glossary of Useful Signs

The graphics in this glossary are used with the permission of the Institute for Disabilities Research and Training, Inc., producers of many fine American Sign Language software products. These graphics are taken from *American Sign Language Clip and Create 2*. This program contains graphics of more than three thousand signs, as well as games and special printing features that allow users to create program materials such as ASL crossword puzzles, posters, and other activity sheets. For more information about this and other American Sign Language software products, see the Institute for Disabilities Research and Training website at www.idrt.com.

Library and School Signs

Group Management Signs

no

Note: This sign is used for the concept of "nothing" or "none," as opposed to the "no" meaning refusal that is found in the Opposites section.

pay attention

please

quiet

share

sit

Animal Signs

cat

caterpillar

chicken

cow

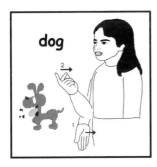

dog

duck

elephant

frog

goat

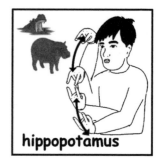

hippopotamus

horse

lion

monkey

moose

mouse

pig

rabbit

seal

sheep

snake

tiger

turkey

People Signs

father

friend

mother

me

my

you

Season Signs

fall

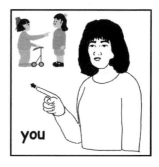

pumpkin

spring

flower

rain

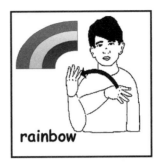

rainbow

summer

sun

winter

snow

star

Color Signs

black

blue

green

orange

pink

purple

red

yellow

Sign Language and Deafness Signs

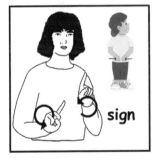

Food Signs

bread

candy

cereal

cheese

chewing gum

cookie

cracker

eat

Playtime Signs

Opposites

yes

no

dirty

clean

same

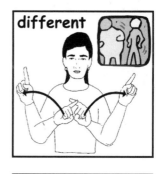

different

true

false

Numbers 1–10

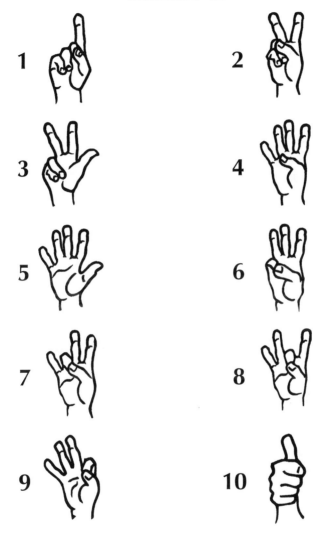

Manual Alphabet

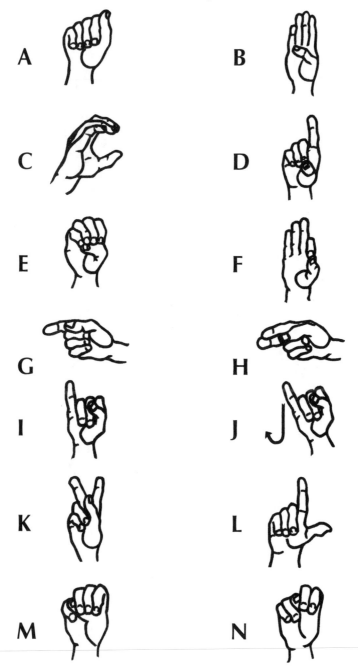

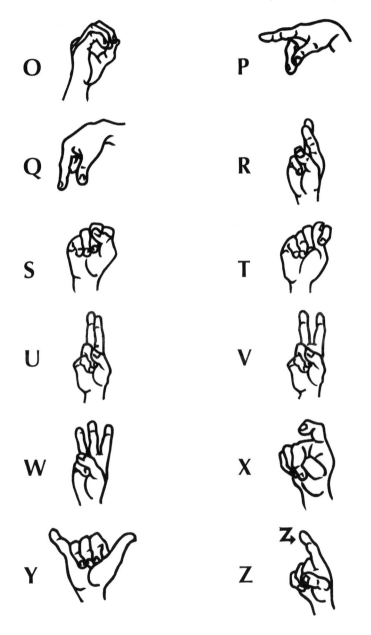

O

P

Q

R

S

T

U

V

W

X

Y

Z

Works Cited

American Heritage Dictionary of the English Language. Boston: Houghton Mifflin, 1992.

American Heritage Stedman's Medical Dictionary. Boston: Houghton Mifflin, 2002.

Gannon, Jack R. "History through Deaf Eyes," at http://depts.gallaudet.edu/deafeyes (accessed December 29, 2004).

Garcia, Joseph. *Sign with Your Baby: How to Communicate with Infants before They Can Speak*. Seattle: Northlight Communications, 1999.

Groce, Nora. *Everyone Here Spoke Sign Language: Hereditary Deafness on Martha's Vineyard*. Cambridge, Mass.: Harvard University Press, 1985.

Hafer, Jan C., and Robert M. Wilson. *Signing for Reading Success*. Washington, D.C.: Kendall Green Publications, 1986.

Lane, Harlan, Robert Hoffmeister, and Ben Bahan. *A Journey into the Deaf-World*. San Diego: DawnSignPress, 1996.

Laurent Clerc National Deaf Education Center. "What Causes Deafness?" at http://clerc center.gallaudet.edu/about/faq.html#deaf4 (accessed December 29, 2004).

Moore, Matthew, and Linda Levitan. *For Hearing People Only*. New York: Deaf Life Press, 1993.

Random House Webster's Unabridged Dictionary. New York: Random House, 1997.

Van Cleve, John Vickrey, and Barry A. Crouch. *A Place of Their Own: Creating the Deaf Community in America*. Washington, D.C.: Gallaudet University Press, 1989.

Wilcox, Sherman. "Universities that Accept ASL in Fulfillment of Foreign Language Requirements," at http://www.unm.edu/~wilcox/ASLFL/univlist/univlist.html (accessed October 18, 2003).

Index

Note: Italic numbers indicate illustrations.

About the Author

Kathy MacMillan is an American Sign Language interpreter, consultant, children's performer, and librarian. She served as library/media specialist at the Maryland School for the Deaf in Columbia, Maryland, from 2001 to 2005. Prior to that, she worked as a public children's librarian for five years, where she developed and presented hundreds of programs for children from birth to age seventeen. Since founding Stories By Hand (www.storiesby hand.com) in 2004, Kathy has presented American Sign Language programs to thousands of children and parents in public libraries throughout Maryland and Virginia. Kathy also presents programming and ASL workshops for libraries, professional associations, and other organizations. During the summers, she directs sign language camps for hearing children and a camp for deaf middle schoolers. Kathy holds an MLS from the University of Maryland at College Park and a certificate in ASL interpreting. She has been a *School Library Journal* reviewer since 1999 and also reviews videos and books for ASL Access. Kathy's articles about library- and deafness-related topics have appeared in *VOYA*, *School Library Journal*, *Public Libraries*, *LibrarySparks*, and *FACES*.